THE DIRECTOR'S EVENT

THE DIRECTOR'S EVENT

INTERVIEWS WITH FIVE AMERICAN FILM-MAKERS

BY ERIC SHERMAN
AND MARTIN RUBIN

BUDD BOETTICHER

PETER BOGDANOVICH

SAMUEL FULLER

ARTHUR PENN

ABRAHAM POLONSKY

ATHENEUM   NEW YORK   1970

FOREWORD

We either like a film or dislike it according to the feelings it gives
us. The nature of these feelings determines the ultimate emotional power
of any film. But feelings in other life experiences create powerful emotional states. How do the feelings we have from watching films differ
from other sets of feelings?

When we watch a film, we perceive its meaning and receive its
feelings by the images thrown upon the screen. The qualities of light,
texture, setting, and geometry all combine to yield certain definite visual
patterns. When these images and patterns are experienced along with a
film's other elements—story, acting personalities, music, etc.—its emotional effect is imparted through our eyes and brain into our body.
Depending on the specific qualities, levels of formal Beauty are expressed
and experienced. So, feelings are expressed with images and these images
are in turn transformed into emotional energies which, due to their
formal Beauty, can affect us profoundly.

We believe that the feelings in a film come from its director. Sometimes, we begin to get similar feelings and perceive similar ideas throughout several films directed by one person. The more we see his films, the
more we realize that he is not telling separate and unrelated stories. We
sense that he is expressing the same personal ideas—images infused with
themes—throughout his works. Because of his films' consistencies, we

v

sense that at some level, he is no longer concerned with isolated effects, but with expressing his own unique view of the world. Finally, this vision comes across more powerfully than any of the actual events or things photographed. The events and things lose their own meaning and come to represent aspects of a director's personal feelings.

For this reason a film—or any work of art—can have a strong impact. We are not so much seeing a story as we are seeing the world through another man's eyes; we are feeling another man's feelings.

Admittedly, these statements are open to question. Perhaps a few examples will help to clarify our ideas and the thoughts expressed in the following interviews. We see a Budd Boetticher Western with Randolph Scott not so much as a shoot-'em-up story as some kind of a morality play. We recognize the Scott character and his quest from other Boetticher Westerns. We feel that he may never quite reach his goals, but we know that he will never stop searching. In fact, the last shots of each Boetticher Western demonstrate that the Scott character can never stop looking. He is defined by his search. Similarly, a Boetticher film from another genre, such as *The Rise and Fall of Legs Diamond,* portrays the same characters and situations. Above all in the shooting of the film, the characters occupy similar positions in the individual shots. A unity of theme is captured not so much in the story and actor as in photography and editing. We are not really seeing a film from another genre, we are seeing the same Boetticher morality play.

We have heard the argument that if its social and political message is not relevant or "right," then a film's value is questionable. This view would be more tenable if a film were strictly a social or political object. But a film is a man's view of the world. If this view is Beautiful (in the formal sense) if it is cosmic and unified, it cannot be rejected *or* accepted. Its meaning is itself. It is in the realm of poetry and music. We cannot reject Samuel Fuller's *Steel Helmet* because a Communist prisoner is brutally slaughtered, or a Buddhist temple desecrated. We are asked to feel Fuller's world in which these events are necessary. Again, when we read in a newspaper or in a history book about an act of brutality, we are repulsed at man's inhumanity. When we see the act in a film, we are repulsed emotionally, but it makes no sense to reject the act, for it exists and has meaning only in the world of that film. A film is more general and more complex than its extracted events. We must react to the unity and Beauty of that film's world.

Even if you agree with these notions, we have heard one final objection, and this concerns the unlikeliness of premeditated artistic seriousness in the highly commercial Hollywood film industry. We reply that it is not a question of likeliness or unlikeliness. Peter Bogdanovich, in his section of this book, says that "Films must be seen and not heard." It is not easy to prove that many Hollywood films are works of art, or that many foreign films are not. The preceding ideas are largely intuitive—as are most ideas about direct human experience and feeling—and emerge primarily after seeing the films themselves. To be receptive to all the power contained in a director's films and their individual images is hard. It takes a certain amount of commitment and willingness to be shaken up. But this is good and necessary, because one man does not easily share his world with another. We hope that the following interviews will at least help to establish these directors' themes and, more importantly, capture a sense of the immediate creative energy and power behind them. We hope that the purpose and final meaning will be implicit in the interviews themselves.

E. S.

ACKNOWLEDGMENTS

For general advice—D. Porter Bibb III, Jeffrey Pollock, Jean-Pierre Jordan, Fred Camper

For use of stills—Ernest Burns of Cinemabilia, Christa Lang, Allied Artists, American International Pictures, Columbia, MGM, Paramount, Twentieth Century Fox, United Artists, Universal Studios, Warner Brothers, Museum of Modern Art, National Screen Service.

For their time, interest, and especially their enthusiasm—Budd Boetticher, Peter Bogdanovich, Samuel Fuller, Arthur Penn, Abraham Polonsky.

All interviews in this book were conducted by the authors except the interview with Arthur Penn, which was conducted by Robert Edelstein and Martin Rubin.

CONTENTS

THE DIRECTOR'S
EVENT

Abraham Polonsky

INTRODUCTION

In 1948, a 39-year-old screenwriter and novelist named Abraham Polonsky directed his first film, *Force of Evil*. Soon after, he was called to testify before the House Un-American Activities Committee and was blacklisted by the movie industry. He disappeared completely from the world of over-the-counter motion picture production. The film he left behind him, although quickly forgotten by amnesiac American critics, indicated the loss of one of the most talented post-Wellesian film-makers.

After twenty years of writing left-wing novels, sub-rosa screenplays, and articles for obscure journals, Polonsky has returned to directing with *Tell Them Willie Boy Is Here,* a major production for Universal Studios. *Willie Boy* confirms that Polonsky's talents have not only remained intact after the bizarre turns of his career, but have matured astonishingly during his enforced inactivity.

The plots of his two films are rigorously simple. In *Force of Evil,*
two brothers, played by John Garfield and Thomas Gomez, see themselves on opposite sides of their corrupt milieu. Garfield, young, ambitious, is the Organization's sweet-talking lawyer who pressures repre-
sentatives of a virtually non-existent law force on the one hand, and
manipulates and consolidates all the cosmopolitan vices for his boss,
Tucker, on the other. Gomez, older, haggard, runs a small-change numbers bank for the simple, honest folk. Garfield tries to force Gomez into

the syndicate. Gomez resists in order to maintain his "honor." Abetted
by a rivalry over Beatrice Pearson, who is as yet uncorrupted, their mutual destruction becomes inevitable.

Willie Boy is based on a historical incident which occurred in 1909.
Willie (Robert Blake), a strong-willed Indian, is intent on removing Lola
(Katherine Ross) from the sterile and dehumanizing Indian reservation.
Coop (Robert Redford), a self-confident sheriff, tries to pacify govern-
ment agent Elizabeth Arnold (Susan Clark), with whom he is engaged
in a love-hate affair, and other white reservation landlords. Willie Boy is
forced to kill Lola's father, and, although it is not considered bad for one
Indian to kill another, it provides a good excuse to eliminate the trouble-

some Willie from the otherwise docile reservation tribes. Coop and a large posse track down Willie and Lola for the remainder of the film. As in *Force of Evil,* the outcome is inevitable.

Within these deceptively simple plot frameworks, Polonsky concentrates on developing a complex series of parallel relationships. These parallels do not really clarify or even contrast one another; they instead create ambiguous and shifting frames of reference. Every aspect of a Polonsky film has a parallel aspect which acts upon the other to create a distorted echo, much like the "murmurs from history" the director refers to in the interview.

In *Force of Evil,* Garfield's major corruption is set alongside Gomez's minor corruption; Beatrice Pearson's suppressed impurity is set

alongside Marie Windsor's open amorality; the vagueness of the criminal Tucker is set alongside the invisibility of Hall, the crusading Special Prosecutor. These relationships induce us to draw parallels which only confuse the issues—we begin to wonder if Gomez's corruption is so minor, if Pearson is as pure as her exterior (*i.e.* the taxicab scene), and whether the force of evil in the film emanates from law or crime. Rather than producing black-and-white contrasts, these parallels tend to merge nihilistically into a mixed ambiguity. The gray dawn of the descent into hell at the end of *Force of Evil* brings us to the point where all imagined values are annihilated, and, like Garfield, we have no other choice but to start over again.

In *Willie Boy,* the development is similar but more extreme. Willie and Lola, the hunted lovers, are paralleled by Coop and Elizabeth, the hunters. In an extraordinary chase which constitutes the major segment of the film, no one really chases anyone. By the first night of the indeterminately long manhunt, Willie and his pursuers are within a few feet of each other. The terms "hunter" and "hunted" become relative. We sense that Willie is passively chasing his destiny, while Coop is actively escaping his.

As in *Force of Evil,* a tension between past and present overlays the more personal frames of reference. In *Force of Evil,* this conflict is almost surreal: the classical decor of the interiors, the references to July 4 and 1776, and the obvious overtones of Cain and Abel clash insanely with a story of gangsterism, the numbers racket, Wall Street, and wire-tapping. *Willie Boy* begins where *Force of Evil* ends. Rather than a surreal opposition of concrete symbols of past and present, *Willie Boy*'s vision of history is stark and barren; only the murmurs are left. The past is realized in the filtered remnants of a dead, mythic Old West: Barry Sullivan's stories of the good old scalphunting days, Willie's relics from his Indian heritage—his ghost shirt and his pagan burial. The present is characterized by several dozen small American flags and a huge, carefully measured chair which await President Taft's arrival; as Polonsky says, "It's so specific that suddenly it's irrelevant." The future is remote; at one point, Willie questions the existence of eternity. When Lola says,

"They'll chase you forever," Willie replies, "How long is that?"

The blankness of the historical framework surrounding the characters, particularly Willie, makes the generalized wish for annihilation more compelling. The merely symbolic death in *Force of Evil,* when Garfield goes "down, down, down . . . to the bottom of the world," is no longer

sufficient. Annihilation must be total. Accordingly, Willie (in a sense) and Lola commit suicide, and Willie's body is burned. In each case, the results are positive: Lola's suicide prolongs Willie's life; Willie's death renders absurd the last great posse, the final enactment of the charade of the Old West; the burning of Willie's body awakens a dormant sense of identity in his fellow Indians. In *Willie Boy,* Polonsky's view of history becomes bleak, apocalyptic—to resolve the ambiguous and immobilizing conflicts between past and present, the past, with all its remnants and relics, must be willfully destroyed. The last line of the film is, "Tell 'em we're all out of souvenirs."

Polonsky's visual style reflects this division of frames of reference. He uses very little middle ground between long-shot and close-up. The long-shots, which presuppose an outer framework (in this sense, they are the more "historical" shots), are rarely shown from the characters' eye-level. One recalls the opening overhead shot of *Force of Evil,* which shows people scurrying like ants in the streets of New York, and the low-angle shots of the Indian reservation in *Willie Boy,* in which the government agent's house seems about to topple over while a huge mountain looms behind it. Appropriately, the characters appear most futile in the long-shots: in *Force of Evil,* Garfield running senselessly down an empty city street, Beatrice Pearson perched awkwardly on a mantle where Garfield has left her stranded; in *Willie Boy,* the high-shots of the posse wandering around, the sense of absurd pantomime in the long-shot of Coop shooting Willie, the final shot of the posse members dancing grotesquely around Willie's funeral pyre. The characters achieve their greatest emotional reality and integrity in close-up—when an outer framework is omitted. The apotheosis of this is the "Garden of Eden" love scene between Willie and Lola, in which the background and foreground are al-

most totally blacked out—by telephoto lens, darkness, and close-up— until Polonsky cuts to a terrifying long-shot of Lola's family closing in on the lovers.

Polonsky's characters are caught between frames of reference which complicate values to the point of producing moral inaction. But when their confusing alternatives are eventually removed, they inevitably slip into the path of a predetermined impulse to destroy the outer frameworks (whether historical, political, or social) which simultaneously create and splinter identities in a modern world. Then, as Polonsky says of Garfield's moral awakening at the end of *Force of Evil,* "There's no problem of identity when you have no identity left at all. In your very next step, you must become something."

The following interview was conducted at Mr. Polonsky's office in Universal Studios, California, in November 1968.

M.R.

INTERVIEW

Polonsky: The trouble with interviews is that everything sounds so damned intended and pompous. It's like someone writing a review of his film after he's made it. A great deal of just plain *living* goes into making a film—that's the pleasure of it—and the interviews never reflect that. They reflect Seriousness and Significance and all that. That's like saying a love affair is all about the time you had these kids. But that's not what it's about, is it? Those are just some of the things that happened. And these interviews always sound like that to me. So, I forgive you, if you forgive me!

I came to make *Force of Evil* because Bob Roberts [the producer] and John Garfield asked me to direct a film. At that time I hadn't the slightest notion that it was possible for me to direct. I'd only written two films: one at Paramount called *Golden Earrings,* which was completely rewritten by Frank Butler, and *Body and Soul,* which was a success of sorts. I had been on the set all the way through *Body and Soul,* and Roberts and Garfield thought it would be an interesting idea if I directed. It was a time of interesting ideas, just after World War II, with plenty of trouble beginning in the United States in political matters. We were all more or less involved with certain radical attitudes and a great sense of loss—who had really won that war?

I knew the novel *Tucker's People* by Ira Wolfert and was fascinated by it. The book had a clear parallel to Fascism. I mean, that's an ordinary metaphor you find in all economic writing and in the poetry of left-wing journalism: gangsterism is like capitalism, or the other way round. I don't know if that's true, but anyhow it's a metaphor when you're desperate.

The great thing about success in Hollywood is that everything you say is considered potentially profitable. So, even though this was a particularly arty subject—arty for a studio film—I proposed it and they accepted it.

I arranged for Ira Wolfert to write the first draft of the screenplay. What he wrote was good, but it was clearly Ira Wolfert writing a screenplay from *his* novel. It's very difficult for a novelist to escape his work, and that would go for me, too, I think, if I were to adapt any of my own novels. Eventually I wrote the screenplay, based on his treatment, the book and our conversations. People who read the screenplay were a little upset by it at first—the language put them off. I know how to write in my own way, but not necessarily in the convention of energetic moving picture dialogue. *Force of Evil* wasn't anything like that and it was a little upsetting to them. But, as I told you, success carries you past all such habitual hesitations. So we made it.

q. Why did you use classical décor in the film, particularly in Tucker's house and in Garfield's office?

a. Why not? The audience immediately accommodates to that as being recognizable, significant, weighty—suggesting power and authority. Therefore, when you come to portray this story, which is actually a destructive analysis of the system, the decor gives you the tension that's necessary to disrupt the given situation.

q. Were you attempting an even broader contrast between the

decor and what was going on inside of it?

    a.   That was the technique of the whole film: unfinished polar re-
lationships. I used the rhythmic line of the dialogue sometimes with the
images, and sometimes against the images. In that Tucker scene when
they are walking down the stairway, the voices are right on mike but the
people are a mile away. I did that all the time. It was the style of the film.

    q.   Another example might be the café scene with Gomez and the

Bauer character [Tucker's bookkeeper]. When Gomez is kidnapped, it's very different from the usual gangster violence. The dramatic and visual tone of the scene was quite muted, and the music was like a religious dirge. In other words, there was a very noticeable air of detachment, of alienation from the images.

a.   You said it! [Laughs.]

q.   Could you go more specifically into why you were trying for this note of disruption?

a.   To create a sense of general anxiety. When you do a thing like that, what you do is utilize the *familiar* as a way of calling attention to the fact that it's not so familiar after all.

q.   Why did you give so much emphasis to that first shot of Garfield and Tucker going down the stairs? In other words, why did you use a long take?

a.   They're on their way to hell, you see. But in the beginning, it looks like they're coming down a grand staircase. It's only later that you find out where they're really going.

q.   So, you intended a definite parallel between that and the final scenes?

a.   "Down, down, down." Right. Also, there's a knocking on the door downstairs, as in *Macbeth,* isn't there? Death is coming! [Knocks twice on desk.]

q.   Another way in which *Force of Evil* differs from the average gangster film is that you never show the Law Crusade. We never see the law enforcement people, particularly that Special Prosecutor, Hall, who is always talked about.

a.   I originally had a scene with the Law, but I eliminated it. After all, who cares about *them?* I mean, with all their talk about law and order, they're not really saying anything. I'm for law enforcement—but not against *me.*

q.   This made the Law much more ambiguous. By making it so remote, you seem to tie it up with the remote fate that these people are dealing with.

a.   The Law is just another representative of the general evil in which we all exist. I mean, it's nice that someone comes and helps you when you're being robbed or beaten up. I like that. But that's not a metaphysical argument. I'd rather have it that *you* helped *me* and didn't have a badge. You just helped me because you saw me suffering, not because you were the Law.

q.   Why did you attach so much importance to telephones throughout the whole film?

a.   Well, first of all, they're useful . . . but they're more than useful. The telephone is a dangerous object. It represents dangerous kinds of things. I don't like instant communication. I like it to take a long time before I understand you and you understand me. In the film, it forms the structure of the characters' relationships. Everybody is tied up with this phone. Garfield makes his call to order the raid, right? And he makes this call a number of times in the film. It's his way of communicating with one world and receiving messages from another. I had a big telephone made so that it would loom very large in the foreground of those close-ups. I guess the telephone was an easy symbol for the connections between all the different worlds in the film. These worlds communicate with each other through telephones instead of feelings. We're getting our messages in *signals,* not *feelings.* Sometimes these messages are correct, and sometimes, even when you hear them, they're incorrect. And to have your telephone tapped, we know now, is the

way we communicate with our government and law enforcement agencies. It's our last means of direct representation except for an occasional riot.

q. In the novel, much more time is given to the character of Tucker. Why is he a shadowy figure in the film?

a. It was necessary for what I was trying to do. The more shadowy Tucker is, the more omnipresent the feeling of what he represents.

q. There seemed to be a direct parallel between Tucker and the Law on the other end of the telephone.

a. Exactly. You see, the people live in a lane, and on both sides of this lane are vast, empty places. On one side, it says LAW, and on the other, it says CRIME. But, in fact, you can't tell one from the other. Except for the messages you get on this phone, it's hard to know. All I can tell is what happens in this lane, and the rest are murmurs from space outside. It's just history talking to us—murmurs from history.

q. How much freedom of choice is there in this lane?

a. Any *single* person can stop anytime, I feel. I don't know if a *thousand* can, but I know any single one can. I believe that. Sometimes, if you stop, you make all the others stop. If you stop believing *that,* you've become the establishment, the organization, the syndicate.

q. Can this one person ever stop outside of corruption?

a. Why not? I don't think the nature of life is to be corrupt. Nor do I think the nature of life is to be good. I mean, the nature of man is to *be there,* as any other animal is there. That's why we invent our moralities. That's the way we handle the world. The fundamental relationship between people is *moral.* That's our social invention—in place of instinct.

q. I wasn't too clear about the man that Bauer meets in front of the bus with a password. Was he a gangster or a lawman?

a. I don't remember. In the film, I have two kinds of people around: cops and gangsters. I don't remember which side this particular person was on, because I made that up as I went along. It wouldn't matter to me whether he was one or the other. I can't remember now what I had in mind with that character. I'd have to see the film again, which I refuse to do because I can only see how bad it is. That film, you know, is fundamentally a failure.

q. The end of the film, where Garfield "returns to society" saying, "I decided to help," is again different from the ending of a normal gangster film. But it also seemed different from the way the story was leading. Do you think this was some real kind of rebirth, or was it the logical development of his character throughout the film?

a. It was a mixture of cop-out . . . and significance. It was a gangster film, and in those days, censorship was much stronger. So, in a way, his last sentence had to say, "I'm going to see that something is done to get rid of all this corruption." People say that to themselves all the time, and I wouldn't consider that, as you must know, a significant remark then or now. That's not the way things happen. How much history do we have to have happen to know that?

So, it was partly a cop-out. It was saying to the censor, "Look. It's O.K. Don't worry about it. He had a change of heart." But that was *completely* on the surface. I didn't mean it at all. What I really meant were all those words at the end and all those images: "Down, down, down."

At the end of the picture, in Garfield's case, it's like being left back in school. I remember in Thomas Mann's *The Magic Mountain,* when he talks about Hans Castorp's youth. Hans is in school, and he gets left back—and what a *relief* it was to get left back! Because *then* you don't have to get ahead anymore. A kind of liberation and freedom comes from failure. What I tried to do there was to get the feeling that, having reached the absolute moral bottom of commitment, there's nothing left to do but commit yourself. There's no longer a problem of identity when you have no identity left at all. So, in your very next step, you must become something.

In general, that's what the ending was: vague. But then changes in personality are always vague. You only know long afterwards whether they had any significance.

q. It seemed to me that you framed the cycle of Garfield's corruption. In other words, at the end of the film, a light is flashing outside the exit of the nightclub when he leaves, and near the beginning of the film, a lot of emphasis is given to the light flashing outside the window of Tucker's office. I interpreted that one as sort of an entrance light, as the other was an exit light. Does Garfield's corruption start right there, which I don't think is true, or, does anything start when he's in Tucker's office at that time?

a. What happens in Tucker's office is not the beginning of his corruption, but that it is called to Garfield's attention. That's the thing. I don't think you begin to get corrupted at any particular moment. You're *already* corrupted when you first begin to notice it.

Life's a kind of corruption, as you live it. Life's a kind of dying, as you live it. You receive messages, as from these telephones, or you receive messages from other people, and slowly you're aware that you're immersed in something. But you don't believe it, because you think you can handle it. And *true* corruption starts at that moment. Because if you realized that you *couldn't* handle it, your corruption would begin to be over. It would be on its way out, wouldn't it? It's that sense of power or control over yourself, that you don't really have, which leads to your tragedy.

q. Thomas Gomez, who played Garfield's brother, felt that he maintained some kind of integrity because he was only involved in small-time corruption, nickel and dime gambling. But Garfield points out to him, truthfully, that they are in some way equal.

    a. Sure. Gomez was even worse; he felt he had an ethical basis. It's even true in American society today. Small businessmen feel ethically superior to trusts, and our laws reflect it. The base of the bourgeois ethic by which we all live in our society is the small businessman. He sits in his shop; he's honest; he deals well; everybody takes advantage of him—and out of him come all the disasters. That's why Tommy Gomez feels he's an honest man; he reflects the whole society.

    q. What about Bauer, the bookkeeper who informs the police? The film gives particular emphasis to his doom. For example, when the numbers bank is raided, there's a shot of him on the floor which is the

exact same shot used when he's killed in the restaurant. Why should we feel that Bauer's more doomed than the other characters, particularly Thomas Gomez?

    a. Gomez thinks he's in charge of his life. Bauer knows he's not. Then, Bauer is an accountant. He has the account books of our society. They balance out, don't they? In the end, one side is equal to the other. God knows what happens in between—which is all this terrible life people lead.

    Bauer is the accountant of the whole picture. Therefore, he feels, "I'm only keeping the books! I'm doing something perfectly proper and reasonable. I do nothing but add numbers. What am I guilty of?" And all the while he feels terrible because he knows he's involved in the whole thing.

A man who feels he's doing something reasonable and who's suddenly caught short is the *perfect* betrayer. You know, if you don't have very strong moral principles, it's hard for you to betray other people. You really have to be committed to do that. That's Bauer.

q.   How does he differ from Thomas Gomez, who also feels that he's not responsible?

a.   Well, Thomas Gomez is in a way like Bauer. But Gomez is the employer. He's carved out this little niche which is fundamentally illegal. And he runs this operation as if it were a human society. He takes care of Doris [Beatrice Pearson]. He takes care of his people. He doesn't want them to get into big trouble. He doesn't want his brother to bring him into the big syndicate and involve him in the *big* corruptions of society. He has this little island of human loyalty, human relations, and benevolence, and that's the way he justifies what he does. It makes him feel like a man, and they want to take away his manhood by making him part of the machine.

So he's different from Bauer, because he's in control. Bauer knows he's in control of nothing, and therefore he never fights. How can he fight? He runs like a rat. That's what he is: a rat, keeping the books.

q.   What is Garfield trying to get out of Gomez?

a. He wants his brother to be his brother—and to forgive everything.

q. Then why does he victimize him?

a. Because he's trying to *save* him. If he just let Gomez go down, Gomez would have no problem. But he's his brother, so he's going to save him—and he kills him. Gomez keeps saying, "Stop trying to save me! You'll kill me! Because you're no good!" This is the classical mythological relationship between these kinds of brothers—all brothers.

q. But does Garfield ever try to destroy Gomez, rather than save him?

a. They're both trying to destroy each other. The older brother, Gomez, had to live a bad life and a hard life, and he says to Garfield, "I made all these sacrifices for *you*. *You* are the favored one, and *you* have the blessing there." It turns out that this blessing is a disaster. The younger brother finds out that you can't do anything with this blessing in the world, except turn it into power. If you turn it into power, you turn it into corruption.

In that sense, you can interpret everything that one person does for another as a way of destroying him. Everything is double-edged in our relations. The way all stories take on their dynamism is that everything has its double nature. You do a thing for this side, and it's the other side that becomes apparent. As you shift from one side to another, one becomes more dominant over the other. Love becomes death and hate— all love, depending on how you make your choices.

In the end, Gomez is doing everything in his power to make sure that his brother destroys him, because *then* his brother is guilty. Garfield says it all the time, doesn't he? "Why are you trying to do this to me? I'm trying to save you! Do you want to make me feel guilty?" And Gomez says, "You *are* guilty!"

q. Even with the classical décor the visual tone of the film seemed stark, almost barren.

a. The cameraman was George Barnes, who, as you know, was probably one of the best cameramen we ever had in this town. He had deep-focus long before other people used it, before Welles and Toland hit it. Now, for years Barnes had been photographing mostly older actresses, making them stay young and beautiful—you know how that's done.

We did a few days' testing and looked at the rushes, and they were beautiful and vague. That is to say, it was the standard romantic photography that he'd been doing, which was absolutely against everything I intended to do in this picture. Jimmy Howe, who photographed *Body and Soul,* doesn't shoot that way at all. He's very clear and precise and naturally anti-romantic. I was used to that, since I'd seen Howe every day on the set of *Body and Soul.*

I tried to tell George what I was looking for, but I couldn't quite describe that to a cameraman, because I didn't know what to say. I went out and got a book of reproductions of Hopper's paintings—Third Avenue, cafeterias, all that back-lighting, and those empty streets. Even

when people are there, you don't see them; somehow the environments dominate the people. I went to Barnes and I said, "This is kind of what I want." "Oh, that!" He knew right away what "that" was, and we had it all the way through the film. He never varied from it once he knew the tone I wanted.

q. The New York exteriors that you used in the film were strange. What were you trying to do with them?

a. Just what you said. I was trying to make strange exteriors.

Just as Tucker's apartment and the offices are full of the nature and power of our society, so are the exteriors full of their beauty and the symbols of their significance: the bank-fronts, the church, the Palisades, the great bridge. Of course, you die at the foot of the bridge, but that happens all the time—we fall off our monuments. We spend our lives falling off our monuments.

    q.   The opening shot of the film shows a huge crowd. As the film

progresses, it becomes less populated, and the final exteriors are deserted.

    a.   Well, by the end, Garfield's flying. He's flying down his dreams or illusions or whatever you want to call them. He's flying to that bridge, and the world gets emptier and emptier. Finally, the only things that are left are his dead brother and this girl—and she's as much a victim as his brother.

One of the scenes that I particularly like takes place after Gomez's numbers bank is raided. Garfield's sitting outside the courtroom, and all these people come out. They have just been let out on bail; everything's arranged. And these people coming out are a freak show, a real one, except for this darling girl. I mean, these people are really beaten. Even if they had had all the success in the world, it's already been stolen from them.

I felt that that scene was shot just the way it should be: the texture of it, the look of it—it's so bedraggled and empty. And then, when Gar-

field meets the girl, I use a romantic image, through the translucent glass doors of the courthouse. Completely romantic—the complete opposite of the milieu. As if to say that you can still hold on to something beautiful and delicious despite everything. Of course you can! That's the cheat. Garfield still thinks so, because he's not finished yet, is he? Going down those steps. I kind of liked that scene. I thought it was successful.

q. Why do you consider the film a failure?

a. Well, it was my first film, and I think there's a difference between what I really intended to do and what came off. I didn't know *how*. And then, despite good reviews, it wasn't a successful picture at the box office. Of course it was a difficult picture, and, of course, it was experimental in a way, deliberately experimental. But, nevertheless, I thought that the general weight of it would be obvious, that people would feel it. But it wasn't felt except by very sophisticated audiences.

q. Did you try to correct these "failures" in *Willie Boy?*

a. *Willie Boy* is totally different. There's no relation between the two films, except as I'm related to both of them. The technique is different. Everything in the world of the film is charged with my meanings, everything is present, you see, so I know I don't have to work so hard to make them available. It'll happen anyway. So it's much simpler . . . *apparently* much simpler. If you wrote a sonata when you were twelve, and then you wrote one when you were fifty, they'd be different, wouldn't they?

q. Could you tell us about your experience with the blacklist? What were you doing between *Force of Evil* and *Willie Boy?*

a. After I finished *Force of Evil,* I went to Europe to write a novel. The blacklist, of course, had begun to operate by then, although it hadn't yet taken on that momentum and destructive energy in the industry. Blacklisting is part of the political behavior of all societies: you put your friends in and keep your enemies out. But it takes on its own momentum, too. It becomes a *thing* with its own life, which has nothing to do with its original intentions.

I'd written this novel, and then I came back here to work at Twentieth-Century Fox. I knew that it would have been safer to stay in Europe—but not really, because not everybody is suited for exile. I think you have to have a temperament for it. Also, the only kinds of exiles that I admire are those who are doing everything in their power to overthrow the government at home, so they can get *back.* Otherwise, you might as well emigrate and get it over with, finish it off and become another person—if they let you.

Now it wasn't that bad—yet. But it was happening. Instead of staying in Europe, I came back here. I was subpoenaed to appear before the committee. I appeared, and was blacklisted.

I made a living all those years mainly by writing for television under pseudonyms. I did a very good show, too, called *You Are There.* At the height of the whole blacklist, a couple of other blacklisted writers and I were doing shows about free speech and personal liberty. You know: Galileo, Milton, Socrates, and so on. But we weren't doing it for that reason; we were just making a living.

Then, by and by, the Hollywood producers started appearing in cloaks and black hats, in obscure corners of remote cities—and giving us jobs fixing up scripts. Very shortly we were making just as much money, if not more, than before, but we were doing infinitely worse work. That was the way the blacklist period was.

I sometimes wonder why I didn't go right down and start working in the underground film movement which was in existence then. I don't know why. It never occurred to me at the time. One of the reasons was:

I didn't want to do any pictures at all . . . I think.

So I turned myself into a writer, in a way. I'd only directed once, right? I didn't consider myself a director. I considered that I *had* directed. But I'd always been a writer of sorts. I became interested in some little, lefty, avant-garde magazine in New York, and I wrote articles for it. The blacklist world slowly ground to a halt with the McCarthy-Army hearings. It did not disappear after the defeat of McCarthy, but it no longer terrorized those people who gave employment. Now they appeared openly. In fact, some of them, like Otto Preminger, just ignored it. He hired Dalton Trumbo and paid no attention to it. Of course, it was soon discovered that if you paid no attention to it, nothing happened. And finally, some three or four years ago, that happened to me.

Frank Rosenberg, who is a producer at Universal, asked me to write a television pilot. Since I had plenty of money at that time, as a blacklisted writer, there was no particular reason for me to do a television show. I was making a good living fixing up rotten movies. So I said, "I'll do it if you put my name on it." In that way, I thought I was getting rid of the possibility of ever having to do it. My name was submitted to whatever the network was. A generally discouraging kind of report came back, which in a sense said, "Get somebody else. Let's not start this up again." When that happened, Jennings Lang, one of the vice-presidents of Universal, called and told the network to go to hell. And they said, "O.K., we'll go to hell." So there I was, able to do that pilot under my own name.

Then Rosenberg prepared the film *Madigan*. The screenplay was being written by Howard Rodman. Rodman and Rosenberg, for their own reasons, didn't get on very well—this happens. So Rosenberg asked me to work on the screenplay. But this was under my own name, you see. After checking with Rodman to make sure that he wouldn't be working on it, I came out here and did some rewriting.

Soon after that, Jennings Lang proposed that I write and direct what we call a "one-twenty," which is a two-hour film for television. Before this, Philip Waxman, who was to be the producer of this television film, had come to me with a book called *Willie Boy*. I proposed that we make it into a "one-twenty." This is not a very good deal for a producer of a "one-twenty" since you get very little money compared with what you get for a feature film. But Lang—he was at the heart of the whole operation as you can see—thought that we could make a feature film out of it. Waxman took his chances. I wrote the script, and they liked it. And I cast it with their help, and they liked it. And I made it, and they liked it. That's the way it happened. Don't ask me if I like it!

q. What was it about *Willie Boy* that particularly interested you?

a. When I read the book originally, I didn't see anything interesting enough in it for me to make a film. I had no particular interest in the Old West or in the New West, or the Old East or the New East, or anything like that. Then, when I was writing *Madigan,* one day I suddenly saw the story, the Willie Boy incident, in a different way. It had nothing to do with the Old West or the New West. It had to do with most of the young people I knew today, living in a transitional period and being driven by circumstances and values they couldn't control. And at that point, I thought it would be an interesting story to do, because then I could play around with this romantic investment we have in the past, along with a lack of comprehension for the realities of the present, and show these two things pushing one way and another. When I saw that, I called up Waxman and said I'd do it.

This picture is intended for young people not yet committed to the disasters of history. If I had one specific intention in my mind, it was to tell my feelings about this to your generation. Not to mine. If mine doesn't know that, to hell with 'em. They should know it by now—and you should know it by now, too. I have a particular feeling about this general problem. Not just because they're Indians, but because this is a general human situation. It's fundamental to human history—this terrible thing that we do. Civilization is the process of despoiling, of *spoliation* of people, which in the past we considered a victory, but we now suspect is a moral defeat for all.

My feeling about this film, in making it, was to address it to your generation and say, "This is what I think about this. This is the way I feel about this. This is the way I see it. This is what this experience is—and you should know it."

By the way, how did you like Bobby Blake, who played Willie Boy? Did you accept him?

q. Completely. I wasn't too sure if Katherine Ross fit into the part of Lola at the beginning, but I think she got better as she got a little more violent.

a. That was the hardest thing in the film. You must accept Blake as an Indian in 1909. I think any first-rate actor can handle most roles, but to look like it, too, is the hardest thing to accomplish. And I think he made it; he actually seems to look like that person, and he certainly

is that person as an actor. Toughest part in the picture.

Ross had the same problem. I mean, how does one become an Indian girl? I tried to overcome that difficulty by making her an Indian girl who wanted to be a white girl. So, wherever she's not really Indian, you say, "Well, that's because she's trying to make it with the whites." Then you finally accept her anomalous position, and she plays into the part. It works out kind of nicely, I think. Of course, you know, in history, no one knows who Lola is, as a person. She's a name from history, that's all.

q.   The grayness of the rocks in the film reminded me of brimstone.

a.   Great rocks, weren't they?

q.   I felt that the film was starting at the end of *Force of Evil,* going down, down, but going far beyond that.

a.   *Force of Evil* dealt more with what they used to call *angst.* This film ignores that. It starts long after we're used to *angst.* It's too serious to worry about generalized metaphysical anxiety. And that's what I meant when I said that I don't want to look at that other picture again. The point of view seems so limited to me.

q.   The chase was handled unusually. You seemed to eschew all melodramatic value—suspense, people catching up to other people, decreasing distance between the pursued and the pursuer, and so on.

a.   Well, I treated it as a formal structure. I took the whole chase and changed it from someone chasing someone to just a formal structure, like writing a fugue, see, so that you wouldn't get mixed up in the pursuit but pay attention to the meaning.

I had it written out originally as a real chase, with events and so on, which you do to make it interesting. Then it occurred to me, just before I started to shoot those scenes, that I didn't really care very much about

27

that. What did that have to do with my story? With what I meant? What I did was reorganize all that into this formal structure. I treated the ambush in that way, too.

q. I had no sense of time throughout the film. This seems unusual for a chase film, where time is usually so important. It was as if time stopped.

a. Well, why do you think that happened?

q. At one point Lola says, "They're white. They'll chase you forever." And Willie says, "How long is that?"

a. ". . . less than you think." It has no duration, has it? Which is why I finally formalized the chase, because if I had used that chase in a dramatic way, I would have brought chronological chase time in and destroyed the picture, I thought.

q. When Willie leaves the Twenty-Nine Palms oasis, several locations are repeated. This gave a great sense of futility to the whole chase; it seemed as if he were retracing his steps. Was this intended?

a. Well, everything is kind of intended. But sometimes intended things have magnificent results in a direction opposite to what you hope for. Then you're happy to see it and take advantage of it. [Laughs.] Hooray for accident! Father of us all!

q. Outside of the four main characters—Blake, Ross, Robert Redford [the sheriff], and Susan Clark [the government agent on the reservation]—everybody else seemed almost irrelevant.

a. Right. But of course everybody's characterized, you see. No one is just a neutral thing, or else the motion picture would be unseeable. But, at the same time, I want these other characters to be the environment, just like the stones, the sky, the water, and everything else—with these four living creatures in it. When many persons are your environment, are within your life, the prime question is one of focus.

q. One character who stood out among the posse was Calvert [Barry Sullivan].

a. He wishes he could live a little again, because everything seems so boring now. Our main use of the Western, in our mythology of pleasure, is to deny its reality and substitute what we like to imagine our history was for what really happened. Everybody does that with history; it makes the present more tenable. So Barry Sullivan plays out this untenable mythological Western, you see. For example, he says to Redford, "Your father was lucky. He died when it was still good to live."

He also says, "I was telling them about the year your daddy and me followed a party of Comanche two hundred miles into Mexico. We brought back six scalps that time." And sitting around that fire with the posse are three Indians! Indian police, who are out chasing this other Indian. The posse members never pay any attention to whether these Indians react to this. All the conversation about Indians, even at the end, is done in the presence of Indians, who are not supposed to have any reality. They're not supposed to think like Indians—they just exist. And we do that all the time, of course, with people whom we think are inferior to ourselves.

But I put in a slow alteration in mood. These Indians finally start to identify with Willie, and then they start to get pretty hostile, and finally Redford says, "Bury him," and they burn him!

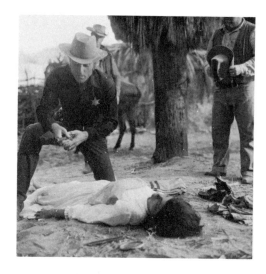

q. The turning point seems to occur when Lola's body is brought up, and the other Indians say that they think she killed herself in order to save Willie, not that she was murdered by Willie. That seems to be where these Indians started to swing over.

a. That's right. And that sort of thing actually happened in history. In real life, unlike in the movie, Willie had committed suicide early in the story. They had twelve posses out looking around for a man who no longer existed.

I used that general feeling of identification, developed between Willie and the other Indians, which arose from the fact that the posse couldn't capture him. Therefore, an Indian was making some kind of stand, in that sense, at a time when Indians made no stands at all. 1890, I think, was Wounded Knee, the last of the Indian massacres. About two hundred Indians, who were wearing those ghost shirts, were wiped out. The Sioux believed if they wore the ghost shirts, white bullets couldn't go through. When Willie runs at the end, you know he's not trying to escape, if you're really tuned in, because he's wearing a ghost shirt. He put his father's ghost shirt on.

Also, Lola killed herself because they would have surely caught Willie if she had stayed with him. Alone he had a chance. Well, instead of making a stand at Twenty-Nine Palms, he really *escaped*. They couldn't catch him; therefore, Lola hadn't died in vain. After that, he was ready to do what he wanted. In other words, she didn't kill herself for nothing: he did escape. But after that, he had no reason to be free anymore.

q. The Susan Clark character, the woman agent on the reservation, was benevolent toward the Indians yet had very little real understanding of the situation.

a. Yes, I think she did a marvelous job of creating the establishment—humanized, but at the same time, infinitely dangerous and infinitely involved. I wanted to show that, despite all of Clark's sympathies for the Indians and her desire to help them, her concern is only with sanitation, education, health. She doesn't have a spiritual concern. She's helping them, and Willie says, "Yeah, she's a helper!" What he means is, "Who wants that kind of help? We don't need any help. We just have to *be*. Our problem is to *become* someone." But Lola doesn't know that until the very end.

We don't really admit the Indians' existence, because their existence means that we don't really belong here. They have no being, except anthropologically.

q. In this light, the only character who "becomes" is Willie Boy. He becomes through his death.

a. That's right. This is a story of an anti-hero, to use popular phrases, who is Redford, and of a real hero, who is Willie. A real hero is someone who fulfills his destiny. And an anti-hero is one who struggles to find his identity in a destiny that he refuses to fulfill. What he's really fighting against is the power structure, the organization, the set-up. Willie is struggling with that, too, but he has a real destiny to fulfill. He's a hero. All he has to do is become himself, and he does. What else can a poor Indian do?

q. In the filming of Willie, it doesn't look like he's making choices along the way. It looks like every step he takes is predestined. On the other hand, every step that Redford takes looks like he's making choices

—the way he carries himself, rides his horse, follows Willie's trail. Willie has laid the trail; Willie is the one who *had to* step there.

    a.   Exactly. And that's what's good about Redford's performance. That's why I called him Coop in the film: Gary Cooper, the great Western sheriff. And he plays this role with a great deal of uneasiness. I think he does it very well.

    q.   When Willie and Lola were making love in the orchard, you cut to a long-shot of the people closing in on them. That was one of the darkest love scenes I'd ever seen.

    a.   It's what happened in the Garden of Eden—after they ate of the tree. It's shot like a Garden of Eden scene. They're completely nude, and yet their nudity is irrelevant. They're not nude; they're in their skins. That's their costume for that scene.

q. You inter-cut a lot between the two love affairs: Willie and Lola, and Coop and the Susan Clark character.

a. I treat both love affairs as a single affair, being acted out by different people at different times. All during the story, that's what it is.

q. The whole thing is who acts out what part. For example, there's an obvious sense of Willie and Lola consummating the affair for the other two people.

a. That's right. That's where the significance comes in. That's the way I make the social significance work without having anything to do with it.

q. All through the film, the town is awaiting a visit from President Taft. The local officials prepare for his arrival by constructing a chair large enough to hold him and by deploying an extravagant number of small American flags all over the place. Again, this seemed to do away with any surface political or social intonations to the story. You see all these flags, and that settles that!

a. [Laughs.] That's it! You see these flags and this immense chair for Taft to fill, and what more can you ask of a President? It's so specific, that suddenly it's irrelevant.

q. About the end, the burning of Willie's body. The posse comes for souvenirs . . .

a. Something to show for all of it! They have to have something to show for all this work they've done—this chase, the money, all this nonsense they've invented.

q. What does Susan Clark's inscrutable expression to Redford at the end mean?

a. Well, ask yourself this question: What do you say to a man who finds himself a prisoner of a situation which he feels he must play out? He feels he must fulfill a role in this situation in order to become a man. And the moment he does so, he realizes that that's precisely the one way he *can't*. In that last scene, he now knows this, and he's washing the blood off his hands. What do you say to him? Nothing. How do you look at him? What do you do? You stay away from him! What does she do? She stays away from him. And that's the end of the film, as far as she's concerned. By the way, while we were filming it, it was Redford who urged this approach.

q. So this man thought he had a job to do, and he thought he

would define himself by doing it . . .

a. Not necessarily to *kill* Willie. Coop didn't go out to kill him, just to capture him. He was *prepared* to kill him. I suppose to be prepared is somehow already to have killed.

q. But he did kill Willie, and in doing so he destroyed himself. But, by the nature of his self-definition, it had to be done. When we were discussing *Force of Evil,* I asked you how much freedom of choice these characters have. Did Coop have a choice *not* to commit this act?

a. Well, he offered Willie and therefore himself the choice to go peacefully, but after Coop had killed him and discovered that Willie's rifle wasn't loaded he knew that there had been no choice after all.

And it's that irony, which is in all events, that defeats all the illusions we have about the choices that we make up for ourselves. *Long* before that event, we have committed ourselves to courses of action which are folly and disaster. And all along the line, we invent choices which we think are real but are just cover-ups.

I think that's the nature of the fake morality that we live by. We invent right and wrong, so that we seem to be making very good choices all the time—and that's a trap! Long before that, we've committed the disaster. And all these choices that we seem to be making are not choices at all.

That's why, long after terrible historical events pass, people say, "But I didn't know!" "I didn't know what was going on in those camps." "I didn't know that was what the war meant." "I didn't know that he was going to die." "I didn't know she was going to be so unhappy." Those are the great *I-didn't-know's.* You've heard them all over. Popular fiction, whether in television, films, novels, or plays, is made of these false *I-didn't-know's.* That's what you call sentimental writing. That's the pornography of feeling. And that's the way we cop-out, to use a favorite phrase of your generation.

q. At the end, these people who are breaking up the fire look extremely desperate and futile. They're not really breaking up anything.

a. No, they're not. They've got nothing to bring back. These Indians burn Willie's body because you could burn the bodies of chiefs in those days. I originally had a line in the script about that, but I took it out—too noble. Now he's burned beyond salvage, and there's nothing to bring back except cinders. So the posse rides in and starts pulling the fire apart—a boot, a shoe, an ear, *anything* to bring back. And they're dancing around this fire, trying to find something. Then Sheriff Wilson goes up to Coop and says, "God damn it, Coop, what've we got to show for it? What will I tell 'em?" And Coop says, "Tell 'em we're all out of souvenirs."

And that's what I want to tell everybody. Never mind all those souvenirs that they keep pushing down on us, all the sacrifices *they* made in the past. I don't care about them. The past is not now. It's just a souvenir, and we shouldn't be bound by souvenirs. If we are, we're not going to live here long. Well, you know that. We're not living here long anyway. They've extended our life expectancy but decreased our chances of living long.

q. Is there any affirmation in this dark ending?

a. Well, we know *they're* in the dark; *we* don't have to be. Willie isn't in the dark. Coop isn't in the dark anymore either, is he?

q. Although Coop may not be in the dark, will his next step be of his own choosing?

a. Far from it. That's why there should be no movement between Redford and Susan Clark at the end that gives you any sense of warmth or affection. It would obscure the ending. It would make you feel, "Oh, well anyhow, Love goes on!" We didn't have anything like that. By then, she knows this man, doesn't she? She comes at Coop's moment of disillusionment, which is Willie's triumph, since he's become himself. And she doesn't do anything. She doesn't weep a single tear, she doesn't show any kindness toward Coop. She just passes him by.

You only kiss returning soldiers in real wars. In these kinds of wars, which, in a certain way, are much more important than real wars, you don't do that. There's no comfort and no company. You're alone, and you want to be alone, and Coop is alone at the end of the story. He walks away from history.

In effect, he says at the end, "It's no use explaining how all these things come about, because all you do is explain. The terrible thing is that they happen." Historical explanations and moral explanations, and explanations of tenderness and love, and *all* such explanations, are irrelevancies beside the fact, as you look at the fact. Now, you look at this fact and face it. I say that to you and anyone. Know this fact and face it.

FILMOGRAPHY

Born December 5, 1910, in New York, New York. Polonsky is one of the three credited screenwriters for *Golden Earrings* (Mitchell Leisen, 1947), although he says that none of his material survived by the time the film was completed. He wrote the original screenplay for *Body and Soul* (Robert Rossen, 1948) and was on the set during the shooting of the film. Polonsky is currently preparing the original screenplay for his next film, which will be called either *Sweet Land* or *Mingo,* and will begin production for Universal Studios in fall 1969.

Force of Evil—1948 (76 minutes)

Producer: Bob Roberts. *Script:* Abraham Polonsky, from the novel *Tucker's People* by Ira Wolfert. *Photography:* George Barnes. *Cast:* John Garfield (Joe Morse), Thomas Gomez (Leo Morse), Beatrice Pearson (Doris Lowry), Roy Roberts (Tucker), Howland Chamberlain (Bauer), Marie Windsor (Edna Tucker).

Tell Them Willie Boy Is Here—1969 (100 minutes)

Producer: Philip Waxman. *Script:* Abraham Polonsky, from the historical study called *Willie Boy: A Desert Manhunt* by Harry Lawton. *Photography:* Conrad Hall. *Cast:* Robert Blake (Willie Boy), Robert Redford (Coop), Katherine Ross (Lola), Susan Clark (Dr. Elizabeth Arnold), Barry Sullivan (Calvert).

Budd Boetticher

INTRODUCTION

The completion of Budd Boetticher's *Arruza* in 1969 concludes an incredible odyssey in the history of American film-making. In 1960, Boetticher, a successful Hollywood director and former bullfighter, went to Mexico to film a documentary about the last stage of the career of his close friend, the great Mexican matador, Carlos Arruza. Seven years later, Boetticher returned from Mexico with the completed footage. In between came a strike, his divorce, a prison sentence, near starvation, a stretch in an insane asylum, a nearly fatal lung ailment, the near loss of the project to John Sturges (who had helped finance it), the death of most of his technical crew, and Arruza's death in a freak automobile accident.

Arruza as a documentary rivals the work of Flaherty. The film begins with Arruza in retirement. He had hoped to challenge the Spanish matador, Manolete, as a climax to his career, but since Manolete has died Arruza has stopped fighting. One day, while riding at his ranch, Arruza chases down a stray bull. He sees that one challenge yet remains for him. He will not only become the first matador of note to become a *rejoneador* (a bullfighter on horseback), but he will become the greatest *rejoneador* in the world. The film traces Arruza's new career and ends with his final, triumphant fight in Plaza Mexico, the world's largest bull-

ring. As Arruza fights the bull, the narrator informs us that Arruza died shortly afterward in a car crash. The narration stops, and the film ends with a breathtaking sequence of Arruza's last performance of his classic art.

    Arruza is the result of the themes and style which Boetticher developed in twenty-five years of film-making. He directed his first film in 1944, at the age of twenty-five. By 1950, he had made ten films, which he signed "Oscar Boetticher, Jr.," and all of which he virtually disowns. In 1951, he made *The Bullfighter and the Lady,* his first bullfighting film and the first film he felt merited the personal signature of "Budd Boetticher." After several years at Universal, where he made as many as five films in 1953, another bullfighting film, *The Magnificent Matador,* and an excellent study of a psychopath, *The Killer Is Loose,* Boetticher emerged as one of the major American directors of the Fifties with his series of seven Randolph Scott Westerns made between 1956 and 1960. The Scott Westerns were followed by a tour de force gangster film, *The Rise and Fall of Legs Diamond.* And then *Arruza.*

A remarkable consistency exists between *Arruza* and the Boetticher films of the late Fifties. As in *Arruza,* grace and stability counterpoint vulnerability to violence and sudden death. Boetticher's style establishes the same delicate balance between ritual, terror, and beauty. His heroes, like Arruza, are involved in an unending quest for honor, which once undertaken cannot be abandoned. The rituals of the *corrida* are a metaphor for the moral code in all of Boetticher's films.

An outstanding example of Boetticher's method is *Comanche Station,* the last of the Scott Westerns. The opening shots of the film show, in long-shot, a lone rider moving through the empty desert. The point of view changes frequently and gracefully, and we see a man

apparently at ease in his environment. As we move closer, however, this relationship dissolves. The desert turns into a foreboding moonscape, inhabited by hostile almost prehistoric savages. Boetticher's films present a seemingly fluid relation between man and his environment which,

like quicksand, gives way under scrutiny. Boetticher's heroes are not so much passing easily through their world as they are constantly in motion, homeless, on the run, but getting nowhere. Accordingly, at moments of dramatic stress, Boetticher's fluid, objective editing becomes subtly fragmentary, subjective. Boetticher's characters, in order to maintain their individuality, remain constantly at odds with their world, which reveals itself treacherously. Many of the most violent moments of *Comanche Station* take place in the most beautiful, peaceful settings (the first Indian attack and Skip Homeier's death by the river), while the most beautiful moments (Richard Rust's story about his father and the final reunion between Nancy Gates and her blind husband) take place in arid, hostile, or dark surroundings.

In opposition to their environment, Boetticher's heroes assign rigid roles for themselves. The director's geometric sense of composition, which fixes each character in a rigid scheme, reflects the moral story he tells. A new dimension is added to the traditional opposition of the Good Guy and the Bad Guy in the Western. In *Comanche Station,* the Bad Guy (Claude Akins) clearly announces his moral position and what it will compel him to do. The Good Guy (Scott) announces, in turn, (a) his moral position, (b) that he knows what Akins will do, and

(c) what he (Scott) will do to stop him. Akins acknowledges that he knows Scott knows, and they proceed to act out, step by step, their assigned roles in the drama they have concocted. This rigidity, this moral simplicity, seems necessary for survival, because those characters (like Akins' assistant, Richard Rust) who vacillate between these clearly defined moral positions, are the first to be exterminated.

The main characters are trapped into their roles, which seem irrevocable. These moral positions cannot be changed by reasoning, because the original reasons behind them, like Scott's wife in *Comanche Station,* seem to have died long ago. We are never given any reasons, social, psychological, or otherwise, why Scott is the Good Guy and Akins the Bad Guy; they simply are what they say they are. Thus, when Scott traps Akins and asks him to give up, Akins replies, "I've come too far to turn back now," and the deadlock can only be resolved by violence. The effect is one of watching a predetermined morality play whose initial impetus is buried in some lost past. *Comanche Station* ends with the same shots with which it began, and we feel that the story will be played over and over. Boetticher's heroes may cover a lot of ground, but they end up, in terms of both miles and morals, exactly where they started.

Arruza, through the nature of his quest and through the ritual and danger he acts out in the bullring, fits into the pattern of Boetticher's heroes. However, in this film, the hero becomes less alienated and more effective in his ritual code of honor because this ethic finds its equivalent in the symbolic world of the bullring. Arruza, once he steps into the *corrida*, becomes one with his environment; he is in a fixed world which he can deal with as he has always dealt with it, and as bullfighters have dealt with it for hundreds of years. In this sense, Arruza is the most positive embodiment of the Boetticher hero. However, Boetticher never lets us forget that the bullring is a different environment from the world around it; this sense is powerfully conveyed in the long-take shot from inside the car which carries Arruza from his home to the dark under-regions of the Plaza Mexico, a zone of shadows which separates the *corrida* from the outside world. After crossing the shadow-line, Arruza

steps out into the brilliant light of the *corrida* for his final fight. The nar-ration, relating Arruza's off-screen death, reminds us that outside the *corrida,* in a world devoid even of the sense of ritual, Arruza died sense-lessly—he was not even driving the car which carried him to his death.

The following interview was conducted at Mr. Boetticher's apart-ment in Hollywood in November 1968 just after *Arruza* had been shown for the first time at the San Francisco Film Festival. Boetticher, of the five directors in this book, is the least inclined to detach himself from his work and contemplate it analytically. The unshakeable yet pragmatic

43

moral tenacity which enabled Boetticher to finish *Arruza* is apparent in his personality and in the heroes of his films, and the two are essentially inseparable. Boetticher is now back in Hollywood, has married again, and has started a new production company with his old colleague Audie Murphy.

M.R.

INTERVIEW

Boetticher: The reason that people understand the Westerns I made with Randy Scott is that they were simple, and in their simplicity I had a couple of goals to reach. I knew where those goals were and what I was striving for. With that in mind, I could put one hundred per cent of whatever talent I had into showing it on the screen. I made *Comanche Station* and *Ride Lonesome* on twelve-day shooting schedules. That's terrible. But I think when you really know what you're doing, you put a lot more into twelve days—artistically, physically, and mentally— than you do into ninety days, just *because* it's impossible. You're really not making a twelve-day picture, because you're giving it twenty-four hours a day.

Nothing in those Scott pictures would make the audience say, "What did he mean? What was he trying to say?" For example, in *Ride Lonesome,** I said a hell of a thing in the last shot. The hang-tree is burning and Randy is standing over to one side. All his frustration is

---

* *Ride Lonesome.* Former sheriff Ben Brigade (Randolph Scott) captures desperado Billy John (James Best) and waits for Billy's brother Frank (Lee Van Cleef) to come and rescue him. Frank had killed Brigade's wife years ago, and Brigade is using his hostage as bait. Meanwhile, Sam Boone (Pernell Roberts) is openly planning to steal Billy John away from Brigade and collect the reward money. Threatening to hang Frank's brother from the same tree on which his wife had been hanged, Brigade draws Frank into the open and defeats him in a gun duel. He allows Boone to have Billy John, and he burns the hanging tree.

44

gone. The point I'm making is that it was done so simply. I said in one shot what I wanted to say: Here is this man's whole life. That tree represents everything bad in his life. And he personally is burning it, having accomplished what he needed to do in order to have the right to light that match.

I said it very simply, and that's the way I make my pictures. One doesn't have to sit there and say, "Well, I don't know . . . ethically . . . and maybe he meant . . ." That's a lot of crap: to be so artis-

tic that you don't make sense. One shouldn't have time to say anything but, "Here comes Randy, and he's alone. What's his problem? Oh, his wife? What happened? Oh, it did? Oooh, seven fellows? He'll get 'em. He's already got three before the picture starts, so he only has four to go, and they're probably in Silver City, because that's where he's headed." You anticipate, and you allow your audience to be with you and to travel vicariously on the same horse with Randy toward what he set out to do.

q. The end of *Ride Lonesome* is one of the few times when the Scott character is able to burn his cross, to fulfill his quest. For example, in *Comanche Station* and *Decision at Sundown,* his position remains unresolved at the end.

a. We wanted his frustration to be satisfied in *Ride Lonesome*. We didn't in the other pictures. I don't really know what happened to the Scott character after the end of *Ride Lonesome*. Undoubtedly, he camped there all night and probably kicked the ashes of that tree in the morning. Maybe he went off to other towns to help the guys who were more or less in the same position that he had been in. Or maybe he just went to a bar and got drunk. I never knew, and I never cared, because when that tree burned, our movie ended.

Ride Lonesome is one of the few stories we could end on the screen. Before, we always let Randy "ride off into the sunset." We always gave you the feeling that there was a tomorrow. I never knew what the tomorrow was in *Ride Lonesome*. I could write fourteen original scripts starting with the burning of that cross.

q. The moral quests of the Scott characters are always determined long before the picture starts, and they will usually go on long after the picture is over.

a. I believe that a picture an hour and a half long is long enough. You can tell the beginning of a story—that's one picture. Or you can tell what I think is the most interesting part of the story—the middle. Or you can tell the end of the story, just as we could start from the ending of *Ride Lonesome* tomorrow. You simply have to choose.

q. Why do you choose the middle section?

a. Because that's where the action is. I establish that something drastic has already happened at the beginning of every one of the Scott pictures. That way, the audience is immediately hooked. Now, if you have to show a peaceful scene in a little village, with the beautiful music and the lovely wife milking a cow and all the junk with the kids, you've got a pretty dull first twenty minutes, if all you want is to show that he loves his wife and she's going to be killed. I'd rather establish the problem right away and then take it from there.

q. At the end of *Decision at Sundown,** Scott says, "Where I

 * *Decision at Sundown.* Tate Kimborough (John Carroll) controls the little town of Sundown with a corrupt but iron hand. Despite a liaison with a devoted mistress, he seeks respectability by marrying Lucy Summerton (Karen Steele), the daughter of a prominent townsman. A stranger, Bart Allison (Randolph Scott), interrupts the wedding ceremony and declares that he will take Kimborough's life by sundown. Allison has been hunting Kimborough for two years to avenge his supposed seduction of his wife, who committed suicide shortly afterward. Sam (Noah Beery, Jr.), Allison's partner, tries un-

come from, folks don't celebrate when a man acts the way he's supposed to." Although the Scott figure is very vulnerable in your films, he has his roots in a certain traditional Western hero, and he represents some sort of an ideal.

a.   Yeah. I think that Randy exemplifies a figure that we have always known as the straight-line hero. You see, he never makes mistakes. However, in the pictures we made together, for example *Comanche Station,** I let you see in his eyes that maybe he thinks Nancy Gates is

successfully to make him face the truth: that Kimborough was only one of his wife's many lovers. Allison is trapped in a livery stable, but his stand inspires the town to turn against Kimborough. When Kimborough finally faces Allison, he is shot in the arm by his mistress, thus rendered unable to draw on Allison. Allison gets drunk in the local saloon and rides out alone at sundown. He saved the town, but was unable to help himself.

    * *Comanche Station.* Every time Jefferson Cody (Randolph Scott) hears that the Indians are ransoming a white woman captive, he buys her back, hoping to find his wife, who was captured ten years ago and is now probably dead. His latest acquisition is Mrs. Lowe (Nancy Gates), whose husband has offered a large reward for her return, dead or alive. At Comanche Station, Cody meets Ben Lane (Claude Akins), who plans to kill both Cody and Mrs. Lowe and collect the reward. Cody finally traps Lane, who refuses to give up

pretty cute, even though he never takes her to bed. I didn't want him to be so inhuman that it looks like he never thinks about it. Then he's not a man at all.

Scott had an obligation to get Nancy Gates home. But, if Nancy's husband wasn't blind, or wasn't there or was a son of a bitch, I think she and Randy would have ended up in Gary Cooper's sleeping bag the next night. I think Randy might have ended up with most of the leading ladies, if they were available. Because if you don't have that going for you, you're a pretty stuffy guy. I thought the Scott character, before the pictures we made with him, was a pretty stuffy guy.

q. The villains in the Scott pictures are very sympathetic. For example, in *The Tall T* Richard Boone is quite appealing.

a. I felt that Boone really loved Randy in the picture, to the point of being terribly attracted to him physically. He would have liked to have been Randy. There's no reason that a man can't love another man. It doesn't have to be a homosexual thing. I think only weak people are afraid of that. If you have a lot of balls, you can say whatever you want.

In every one of the Scott pictures, I felt that I could have traded Randy's part with the villain's. Before, in Westerns, the hero always shot the villain and gloated. In *Seven Men from Now,** after Scott is forced to shoot Lee Marvin, he sits down on a rock and mentally vomits. Scott didn't want to shoot him. He liked Marvin. But he had to.

q. In your Westerns, the hero and the villain seem locked into

---

and kills him. Although he had questioned the honor of a husband who would not try to personally retrieve his wife, Cody discovers, when he returns Mrs. Lowe to her home, that her husband is blind, and he leaves.

* *Seven Men from Now.* Seven men led by the notorious Masters (Lee Marvin) rob a Wells Fargo office and kill the wife of former sheriff Ben Stride (Randolph Scott). Stride vows revenge and accompanies the Greers (Walter Reed and Gail Russell) to Silver City, where Masters is holed up and where John Greer is going to deliver the Wells Fargo gold he has hidden in his wagon. Greer, ashamed when he encounters Stride's moral fortitude, decides to stand up to Masters. He is killed, but Stride defeats Masters in a final showdown over the box of gold.

their moral positions. For example, in *Comanche Station,* when Scott asks Claude Akins, the villain, to give up because he doesn't have a chance, Akins says, "I've come too far to turn back now," and they shoot it out.

a. That was more or less the same ending that we used with Marvin in *Seven Men from Now,* and with Boone in *The Tall T.* It had to happen. You can't back away from a situation like that. I've just returned from seven years in Mexico, and everyone wanted to know why in the hell I didn't back out of *that* situation.

q. Why does Boone come back and try to kill Scott at the end of *The Tall T?** Could he have kept going and escaped the situation?

a. I think he had to come back. When Boone gets wrapped up in that burlap outside the cave, so that he can't even see, it's like putting a hood over Susan Hayward's head in *I Want To Live.* No matter how many steps you have to take, when they cover your head up, you're dead.

Also, remember that Boone's last cry was for Randy. In dying, he wanted to see him. By the way, I stole that scene from myself. In *The Bullfighter and the Lady,†* Gilbert Roland dies before Bob Stack

* *The Tall T.* Arizona rancher Pat Brennan (Randolph Scott) is held hostage along with the wealthy Doretta Mims (Maureen O'Sullivan) and her freeloader husband (John Hubbard). Their captors, outlaw Frank Usher (Richard Boone) and his two paid killers (Henry Silva and Skip Homeier), murder the husband when he tries to doublecross them all. Usher rides off to collect the ransom money from Doretta's father, leaving his two assistants behind. When he returns and finds his cohorts killed, he proposes a truce to Brennan. Usher starts to ride off, but is compelled to return to Brennan, who kills him.

† *The Bullfighter and the Lady.* Chuck Regan (Robert Stack), a champion skeet shooter, travels to Mexico and decides to try his hand at bullfighting. He is instructed by Manolo Estrada (Gilbert Roland), one of the great matadors. Unsatisfied with Estrada's classical, methodical approach, Regan wants to leap ahead to the big *corrida.* In his first big fight, he is about to be gored by a bull when Estrada saves him. Estrada is gored instead and dies before Regan can speak to him. Now the most unpopular bullfighter in the country, Regan must prove himself again in the bullring.

has a chance to say he's sorry. The terrible thing is that he never got to apologize. In *The Tall T,* the situation with Boone is that he really adored Randy Scott. If Scott hadn't had to kill him, Boone might have turned into a fine guy. But he didn't even get to say goodbye!

Boone had to return to Randy for his own honor, because a guy without honor isn't even going to get to be a Legs Diamond. You may be as immoral as hell, but you have to have perseverance in what you believe to become a great immoralist. All of my villains have definite ideas about what they want to do. They may realize halfway through their association with Scott that they're wrong, but by then they're too far committed. They're past the point of no return. That's why, morally, Boone had to come back, maybe knowing that he was going to die. He was a kamikaze pilot; he saw a battleship, and he had to take a chance.

q.   Does this code of honor relate to why you often have a middle-of-the-road character—like Walter Reed in *Seven Men from Now* —who gets caught in between and realizes he's without the code?

a.   Well, he's the average man. That's why we put Reed in the wagon: he's not going any place. Look at his wishy-washiness during the scene with Lee Marvin in the covered wagon. Marvin tells Randy that he'd like Reed's wife. If Reed hadn't been wishy-washy then, he would have been shot by two professional gunslingers. So he'd better stick to the middle of the road.

q. Even though these characters vacillate in order to survive, they're usually the first ones to die in your pictures. For example, in *Comanche Station,* the minute Richard Rust starts to waver, he's doomed.

a. That's probably a tremendous comment on my own attitude toward life. I haven't time for wavering. I haven't time for wishy-washy producers and writers. A producer asked me about one of my scripts yesterday. He said, "Do you like it?" I said, "What do you mean—do I like it? I love it, or else you wouldn't be able to read it!" I've had writers come to me with their scripts and say, "Gee, I'd sure like to know what you think." I say, "Well, what do *you* think?" "Well . . . I don't know." "Then take it home! And when you just love it, bring it back. But don't bother me with something you're not sure of."

I hate insecurity. Although I never thought of it before, I probably don't like those middle-of-the-road characters in my films, so I get rid of them. I get rid of all those friends around me, too. Boy, the minute I sense that—whap! Cut off their heads! And you can cut off a man's head, as I have done in Mexico, when you're cold and hungry and without a penny, if you still have some moral integrity.

q. I love the scene in *Comanche Station* where Rust tells Skip Homeier the story about how his father always said, "A man's got to amount to something." You often have humorous interludes in your Westerns.

a. I think I lend a lot of humor to my films, because I'm always having such a good time. It's very difficult for me to work eight hours a day without doing something I think is funny. We have the same type of scene in *The Tall T,* when the two kids are sitting outside drinking coffee and talking about the whorehouse. We have it in *Ride Lonesome,* when they're sitting out by the tree and talking about the scalps. We even have it in *Buchanan Rides Alone,** when Craig Stevens is standing on the bridge with all the bodies around him, and he says, "Don't just

* *Buchanan Rides Alone.* Buchanan (Randolph Scott) rides into Agryville, a town ruled and largely inhabited by the Agry family. Juan de la Vega (Manuel Rojas), son of a wealthy Mexican landowner, guns down one of the Agrys, who had raped his sister. Buchanan tries to help de la Vega, both are apprehended, and the town wants them to hang. However, the politically ambitious Simon Agry (Tol Avery) decides it is more expedient to ransom de la Vega. Interfamilial bickering and greed allow Buchanan and de la Vega to escape. In a climactic gunfight over the ransom money, a large portion of the stand there. Go get a shovel!"

You know, there are only a few things you can make an audience do. You can make them terribly angry, or you can frighten them, or you can make them cry (which is easy), or you can make them laugh, which is very hard, because today they just sit there and say, "O.K. Be funny." Those are the only four things I ever want to do. I think that if directors want to teach a lesson, they ought to do it at the University of Southern California or UCLA. Don't force us to see it in a movie, because we don't have time to absorb it anyway.

q.   The exteriors in your Scott pictures are fresh and original. This must be hard to get in a Western nowadays.

a.   I agree with you. Most of our locations were found on horseback. I and Lucien Ballard, my cameraman, would get on our horses and ride up to where you just couldn't go. Then a helicopter or an assistant director on a pogo stick would find us, and we'd say, "Here's the location. It's up to you to figure out how to get the trucks in." Then they'd dynamite, move boulders, build roads, and so on.

I once had a very funny experience about that. Lucien and I bundled up and got on our horses about four o'clock in the morning. It was for the opening of *Comanche Station.* We rode and rode and rode up this mountain, and we found a location just before the sun came up. I said, "Lucien, if we put the camera right here at exactly this moment tomorrow morning and bring Randy right down there, we have a great title shot!" He said, "Yep, it always was." I said, "What do you mean?" He said, "Raoul Walsh* and I did that same shot eleven years ago." And we moved over about four feet and dug in the sand, and there was a spike that Raoul Walsh had put there!

q.   In that opening of *Comanche Station,* the Indians look and communicate almost like cavemen.

a.   That's what they were. You know, people have forgotten one

---

town's population is exterminated, but Buchanan saves de la Vega's life as well as his money.

* American director, dean of action pictures such as *They Died with Their Boots On* and *Gentleman Jim.*

thing about the West: these were very simple people. They didn't use words like "gregarious." They didn't have a big vocabulary. You see these psychological Westerns today, by some of these new directors who won't be around very long, and the characters are talking (if you'll pardon the expression) like Yale students.

These people didn't have that kind of an education. They weren't necessarily "Yep" and "Nope" and "Mebbe" men, but they didn't speak the way people speak today. When you have people who can't make themselves understood in a sophisticated way, they also don't have very intricate thoughts. Their thoughts are pretty simple: "That's mah wife, and she's in trouble, and Ah'm gonna get her." What comes between him and his wife is a serious thing, and that's your story. The villain's attitude is: "Ah want that fellow's wife, and he's a-comin', and Ah've gotta kill him." That's your villain. You can't be as articulate as hell and make pictures about these characters. You've got to understand them.

q. Legs Diamond* is in some ways similar to the heroes in your Scott pictures. Usually, in a movie, when a gangster goes to the top, he has a big organization and many henchmen. But Legs, like Scott, works alone; he's a one-man terrorist organization.

a. He was a loner. He was a complete loner.

q. Like some of the villains in the Scott pictures, Legs is also quite charming.

---

* *The Rise and Fall of Legs Diamond*. Jack "Legs" Diamond (Ray Danton), a petty crook, insinuates himself as one of Arnold Rothstein's (Robert Lowery) bodyguards. After a near fatal shooting, Legs circulates the legend that "the bullet hasn't been made that can kill Legs Diamond." When Rothstein is killed and his domain is being divided by other leading gangsters, Legs moves in. His demands are simple: "Give me fifty per cent of the take, or I'll kill you all." After several killings, the gangsters are convinced. Legs leaves for a trip to Europe with his dipsomaniac wife (Karen Steele). They spend most of their time in movie theaters watching newsreels which depict the end of the Twenties and the gangster era. Legs returns to find crime controlled by a huge organization. He tries to enforce his old terms, but the new breed tells him, "What can you do? Kill us all?" Legs' magic is gone. He is betrayed by a former mistress and gunned down in a hotel room.

    a. I made *Legs Diamond* because I had a feeling I could make a gangster picture that was completely different from any other: it had a sense of humor.

I interviewed, without knowing their names, quite a few hoods in New York, Chicago, and Detroit. I'd go into a local bar or restaurant and they'd spot me. Two fancily dressed young men would come up and say, "Mr. Boetticher?" When they said "Boetticher," I knew they knew me, because even my mother couldn't pronounce that name. They'd sit down, have a Coke or a lemonade, and say, "We understand you're going to make a picture about Jack." I'd say, "Well, I'm gonna try." They said, "What kind of picture do you want to make?" I said, "Well, I don't think that anyone who reached the top, even in gangdom, had to be all bad. He must have had something, even if it was a sadistic sense of humor, but something I can pin a motion picture on. Now, the guy may have been a son of a bitch, and undoubtedly was from what I've learned, but I want people to care when he's killed." Then they'd say, "Are you really going to make that kind of a picture?" I said, "Yeah, I'm going to try." Well, after hearing that, they gave me all the information I needed, and I was able to make Legs a very charming character.

q. How did you get the grainy, documentary look in the photography of *Legs Diamond?*

a. You're talking about my favorite cameraman. If I could have Lucien Ballard on every picture, we could lick the world. It's very difficult to be a "bad" cameraman on purpose, like Lucien was in *Legs Diamond.* We deliberately made our film stock look old and grainy. We pre-exposed it a little bit, and it looked awful. At certain points in the film, it's impossible to tell which is the footage we shot and which is stock film from that period. That's exactly what we wanted.

When we started the picture, Lucien and I ran a lot of gangster pictures from the Twenties and Thirties. We found out many things that I didn't know. They never used any foreground pieces then. They didn't dolly. Naturally, they didn't zoom. Most importantly, they didn't compensate for blondness or darkness. That's why I used Ray Danton and Karen Steele as my stars. In one scene between them, we wouldn't compensate for his darkness, and she'd be overlit. In the next scene, we wouldn't compensate for her blondness, and he'd black out.

I didn't like working with our producer on that film. He thought we were really shooting junk. On the third day of the picture, he came up to me and said, "I thought you said that Lucien Ballard was a great cameraman." I said, "He's a genius!" He said, "But, good God, this stuff

looks like it was shot in 1920!" Well, how do you compete with that? So I just said, "Go away. Let us finish the picture."

He went to Jack Warner one day, and he said, "J.L., you know what that son of a bitch told me to do?" Warner said, "What son of a bitch?" He said, "Budd Boetticher!" Warner said, "What did he tell you to do?" "He told me to go to Palm Springs until the picture is finished." And Warner said, "Where are you going to stay?" That's how we were able to finish *The Rise and Fall of Legs Diamond.*

q. In terms of the script, Legs' fall comes about because everyone who loved him has left him. In terms of the documentary style of the film, the fact that his world has left him is a stronger reason. The parallel between the newsreels, depicting the end of the gangster era, and the shooting style of the earlier part of the film seems to clinch this point.

a. Right, but we had to personalize the ending with his wife. We had to go a little Hollywood, which is why I'm not crazy about that picture. But we did hit in the newsreel montage that his world had left him.

q. When you first went down to Mexico to make *Arruza,* did you know that you'd have to go it alone, or did you try to get some outside financing?

a. I went to Jack Warner, who's a dear guy to me. All the really tough men in Hollywood, who are supposed to be bastards, have been my friends. The well-polished, manicured, polite, artistically well-hung executives—those are the sons of bitches you have to worry about. But the Cohns and the Goldwyns and the Warners and the Mayers—these are the *men.* I went to Warner, and he said, "Look, I like the idea. I'll give you three million dollars—if you use Tony Curtis." I'm not being facetious. That was the deal.

I had made *Bullfighter and the Lady* with Bob Stack and Gilbert Roland, and I loved Tony Quinn in *The Magnificent Matador.* But, having been so close to bullfighting, I hated the idea that Bob Stack or Tony Quinn or Gilbert Roland shakes his cape, goes *"Hé, hé,"* and then you cut to a long-shot, and Tony Velásquez or some other double makes the pass.

I had the choice of doing the life of Luis Miguel Dominguín in Spain, or Arruza in Mexico. I waited for two years, and I weighed which way to go. Fortunately, artistically I chose the tough way—without knowing it. But when Carlos decided to become a *rejoneador* I knew I had made the right choice. If I had gone broke in Spain, Luis Miguel would have written me a check for $200,000. Arruza never put up $2.27. But he was a genius.

I've got to tell you one story. While I was shooting *Arruza,* I taught school at the University of Mexico—an "unpretentious" subject called Cinema. You know, that's like teaching Catholicism. Where do you start? At any rate, at the end of the semester, one boy came up to me who was pro-Budd Boetticher and against all the years he thought I had wasted in Mexico. He asked me how I could leave everything in the world for one man. I had never thought of the answer before. At first, I thought it was a moral issue. Then I thought it was a financial thing. Then I thought maybe I was fighting Hollywood, and doing what I wanted to do artistically with a little—well, in Spanish, the word is "category"—I guess here you'd say integrity. And then, in one second, it came to me. I said to him, "Wouldn't it have been a wonderful thing if the director of *The Agony and the Ecstasy* had Michelangelo instead of Charlton Heston?"

I had my own private genius for eight years, who did what I wanted, stood where I asked him to, walked out in the sun to be in the light, and fought the bulls to the best of his ability right in front of every one of my cameras. You don't get that very often in a career.

Yeah, I thought I'd have trouble, but I had no idea I'd have so much. I thought it might take six months with bad luck, and a year with dreadful luck. The way it turned out, though, proved to be very interesting and very educational. The seven days I spent in prison were the most fascinating seven days of my life. It was a great experience. When you're very young, and you're broke and hungry and living in a cold-water flat, you can rationalize and say, "Well, what the hell? Everybody started that way." But it's a different thing when you've already been successful and wealthy and have had everything. I was the only director I know of in the world who went from a new Rolls Royce to a bus—and it was kind of charming. I remember every ride in those damn Mexican buses. When you lose everything in your forties, you remember each minute, each second. People who were in Mexico at the time have read my book and said, "How did you remember that?" Jesus, how could I forget it? It was like a seven-year, dreadfully slow, and horribly painful movie—with a lot of very funny incidents.

In the long run, I now have a much better concept of what I want to do. I sure as hell understand people a lot better. I was terribly hungry and terribly cold, but I'm delighted things turned out like they did, because I remember those times now.

I don't think you can improve on *Arruza* as a documentary, and that's what I set out to do. You know, ordinarily a director makes ten documentaries—*How to Shift a Formula One, How to Drive a Nail, How to Hang a Picture*—and then he makes a feature. If you've made thirty-one features, and *then* you make a documentary, you sure as hell should have learned something. If I have, it's all in *Arruza*.

q. When you were in Mexico, were you ever tempted to give up and come back to do another Western?

a. Never. I was very much in love with a wonderful girl. She's in my book; I call her "Artis." I had to make a decision. I was dead broke, with nothing but whatever talent I have. I could either let her go home to Chicago, or I could marry her and burden her with the responsibility of an unemployed director. One day, I said, "Honey, let me explain one thing to you. I love you. But if I marry you, and because I love you, and because I have a responsibility to support you, I have to do *Batman* one day, I'll hate your guts in six months." Which is true. You must have artistic integrity. No, I never would have quit. I damn near died a couple of times, and at times it was impossible to continue, but I couldn't quit.

Once when I was boxing in college, I was getting the hell kicked out of me, I thought. I was the only one, as far as I was concerned, who was getting hit. I had a cracked nose and a couple of black eyes. Between rounds, I turned to my coach and said, "I can't make it through the next round." He said, *"You* can't? Look across the ring! Do you think he can get up?" The fellow I was fighting was in much worse shape than I, and I eventually won.

That taught me a hell of a lesson that I've learned about pictures and, I think, about life: everybody wants to quit. Probably during Lindbergh's flight across the Atlantic, he thought, "If I go another ten miles, I'm at the point of no return. I'm going to have to go on, and I don't want to. It's cold up here." I don't care who you are, or how brave you are, at one point you have to want to quit. If you just make up your mind that you're not going to quit, ninety-nine per cent of the people around you will quit, because it's so easy, and you'll win.

That's the attitude I had all the way through *Arruza.* Many nights in a little Mexican village I was cold and really hungry. I had a charge account—I think the only one in history—with a tamale vendor. You could get a *dulce* (sweet) and a *rojo* (red) and a *verde* (green) tamale for one peso. That's eight cents. You get three of them. That would be my evening meal. I had to eat something. I drank a lot of water, and, with all the corn that goes into the tamales, I could kind of exist. I ran up a 190-peso bill. At a peso a day, that's a lot of time! Then I got a residual check, after many years, for the pilot of *Maverick* that I directed. It was for some $700. I finally paid this guy his 190 pesos in one lump sum. It took me a week to find him. It cost me 200 pesos to get him out of jail! He just went crazy. He'd never seen so much money. He bought all the tequila in this little town and stayed drunk. So my residual was depleted very quickly on my friends. But it was a great experience. Now I think there's a chance I might be a good director. I've certainly had the background in the last seven years!

q. Did those seven years ever threaten to seriously disable you, physically or mentally?

a. Sometimes. I'll tell you what I did. I had a system. Five different times in the seven years in Mexico, I just locked myself up when I thought I would have to go to a psychiatrist or lose my mind or start to scream. I'd get about four or five bottles of tequila and a lot of beer. Then I'd close the door and just get stoned for two or three days. I'd

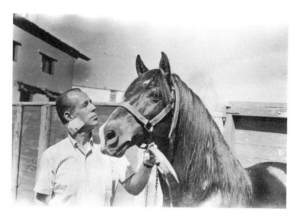

Boetticher in Mexico (after being gored in the neck by a bull) with his favorite horse.

wake up and feel awful, because I don't drink, and then I'd start over for another six months of hard labor and mental anguish. That way, it never got to me. I found it was a great catharsis. I can't recommend it, because if I hadn't had a strong heart, I would have died of a heart attack many times.

Also, during *Arruza,* I kept thinking, "Maybe I'm going to die." This worried me very much, because I had nineteen hours of footage, and I was the only one who could put it together right. In fact, I'm the only one from that film who's alive today. My cameraman, my cutter, three grips, two electricians, Carlos—they're all gone.

One interesting thing about that picture, cutting-wise, is that I went to Mrs. Arruza eight months after Carlos was dead. I said, "Mari, I want you to play Mrs. Arruza." She said, "Why should I play Mrs. Arruza?" I said, "Who are you?" She said, "Mari Arruza." And she did the picture eight months after he was dead. Some of the shots in those sequences between Mari and Carlos were done five and six years apart, but they're beautiful.

    q. Is it true that you photographed much of Arruza yourself?

    a. I had to, because I knew the bulls. I put the camera where

I knew things were going to happen, because I was a bullfighter. You can't have a cameraman trying to follow a bull that's wide open. So the combination of being a *torero* and a fairly accomplished director have made what I consider a great motion picture.

The wonderful attitude I have about this film is that if people don't like it, they're wrong! I got one bad review in San Francisco that said it was a great film for *aficionados,* but otherwise it was dull. And it killed me! Everybody said, "What do you care? He said it was a great picture for *aficionados."* But it killed me that he said it was dull! It broke my heart, because I made the picture for bullfight fans, but—damn it—I don't want to lose my grandmother if she doesn't like bullfighting. She should come out of it and say, "I don't like it, but it's beautiful."

Peter Bogdanovich and I were talking the other day about reviews: if you get twenty-five good reviews, and the twenty-sixth says you're lousy—that's the review you can quote! For instance, someone said about my first picture, "This wasn't released; it escaped." That was twenty-four years ago. I remember that line today and will die remembering it! Those are the ones that hurt.

q. What did John Sturges have to do with *Arruza?*

a. John Sturges, a fine director, bought into my picture. He thought I was wrong and he wanted to recut it. Of course, he didn't cut one goddamned frame! I had to take out my contract and say, "Read page four—'Artistic control: Budd Boetticher'!" Sturges thought the picture was slow; he thought that it was old-fashioned. *Arruza* is "old-fashioned" because I realized that it would be history. I didn't want any *Bonnie and Clyde* tricks that in ten years would make people say, "Well, they must have shot this in 1960, because that was the vogue."

I wanted *Arruza* to be pure. There's no dialogue in it at all. It would have been lovely if Carlos had said something, but they would have been my words. That would have been phony. Now the narrator says, "This man is the best. This is what he does. These are the horses, and those are the bulls. And he's dead." That's the story. We give you a little bit on how to ride a horse, but not much.

I did not compromise on *any* shot in *Arruza.* And I still sit in the theater and cry a little and love it and shout "Olé" at my friend. So *I* cut *Arruza*. Right or wrong, that's it. If there are any awards, God willing— and on this picture, God must have been willing—I'll accept them, and if there's anything wrong, I've got to take the blame. It's a very healthy situation to finally have arrived at where it's really your fault, good or bad.

q. What do you think your standing is in Hollywood after having been away so long? Do you think the production system has changed to the point where you might have difficulty readjusting?

a. I think I've been gone during the period when Hollywood took a chance on a lot of young, inexperienced talent. A very small percentage of them actually had talent. Now, I don't think I'll have to fight as hard, because they'll think I'm sixty-five years old when they look at how long I've been directing. I started to direct when I was twenty-five. So I think that if I make a couple of good pictures, there won't be many fights. It should be a comparatively easy road in the future.

I may be wrong, and if I do have to fight, I'm sure as hell equipped for it. As I wrote in my book, Hollywood looks like Disneyland compared to Mexico. This is kid's stuff up here. Down there, they're for real. When they say you're dead, you're dead—with a gun. When they tell you they're going to put you in jail, that's not a threat; you find out you're there after you're in. So this should be a comparatively easy portion of my life—with any luck. But my life's always been exciting, so maybe it'll be the worst period of my life!

I really want to get back to making Westerns. They have a fine screenplay of mine that Clint Eastwood and Shirley MacLaine are doing at Universal. It's called *Two Mules for Sister Sara*. Originally, I was signed to direct. Now they've hired Don Siegel, and they want to pay me off. It's awfully tough to write a script and fall in love with the characters, and then have somebody else direct it. No matter how good Don is, he'd be the first to admit that I should've made it. I guess all these things add up to why I'm suing Universal for $4,000,000. The pay-off offer was all right, but nothing compared to what I deserve.

I have another story that I'm writing now called *A Horse for Mr.*

Barnum. It's very funny, and it'll be made in Spain. I always wanted to make a picture in Europe, not to take advantage of it, but to use it. *A Horse for Mr. Barnum* is a Western that takes place in 1880—with castles! You don't have to put a bush in front of a castle that's in the background, because you're in Spain, not Texas. It's a lovely story. It's about four guys—like McQueen and Boone and Marvin and Coburn—who have met because each has answered a mail-order ad in Sears and Roebuck by a guy named Phineas T. Barnum to go to Spain and pick up a hundred head of white Andalusian horses for the Barnum and Bailey Circus. And they just fuck up Spain. They're really there, and they're out of place, and it's horrible, the things they do to Spain. I'll love making it.

The very next thing I'll do starts in March 1969 with Audie Murphy as producer. It's called *A Time for Dying.* I kill off the young leading man at the end of the picture. They're a little shocked about that, because he's such a good guy. He's not Clyde of *Bonnie and Clyde.* He's a great guy. But he just doesn't have it. This is a Western about all the un-marked graves, about all the kids who had everything but just didn't win. It's a terrible thing—all the teenage kids who wanted to be Billy the Kid or Jesse James, and they don't even have a marker on their graves. You can't even find the holes they're buried in, and they're all over the West. These kids who got shot are like the young bullfighters who never get into Plaza Mexico. They get killed or wounded or frightened to death before they ever get in the big bullring. It should be quite a film for today's youth—a real indictment against stupidity.

You know, at one point while I was making *Arruza,* some people wanted me to come to Spain and make *A Time for Dying.* I'll never for-get the scene. I wouldn't dare put it in a picture, because nobody would believe it. One morning, I was eating one of my tamales, saving one for lunch and the other one for dinner. I got a special-delivery, air-mail, registered letter from Madrid. They offered me an exorbitant salary, a chalet outside of Madrid with a swimming pool, a penthouse in Madrid, and $750 a week expenses to do the script. I was in the middle of *Arruza,* starving to death, and I couldn't go. I never answered the letter.

65

They must have thought I was out of my Chinese head. But I couldn't go, because I already had more invested in *Arruza* than I would have made in three of those pictures. You just can't write all of that in a letter. So I sat there, and I looked at this one tamale. I nearly ate the other two, just to splurge—on the money I was turning down!

q. Now you want to go back to making Westerns. Some people might feel that now that you have some security, you should shoot an Important Subject film, on the Atom Bomb or God's Silence. They don't understand that somebody can express himself to the utmost of his ability in a low-budget Western.

a. Let me explain something to you. I'm a very happy guy. I know where I'm right, and I know where I'm wrong. I never fool myself. I'll always do what I please, because what I please to do I understand. I know Westerns. I know bullfighting. I know athletics. And I know a certain moral story.

I want to film my book someday.* It's called *When in Disgrace,* and it's based on my experiences in Mexico. It would be a fantastic picture. I can't make it in Mexico. It would be real. Everything's in it.

My agent called me one day, and he said, "Listen, I just finished reading your book. It's fantastic, but can I ask you a personal question? Now don't get upset. Didn't you kind of build some of that stuff? I mean, it's kind of hard to believe." I said, "Let me ask you a question. If I wrote you a screenplay about a comparatively successful director who married a motion picture star who was gorgeous and beautiful, and they bought a Rolls Royce, and he invested all his money in a picture, and they went to Mexico to make the story of his best friend's life, and the motion picture actress and the director were divorced because of the picture, and he lost his Rolls Royce, and he spent seven days in prison, five days in an insane asylum, and he was given up for dead for four days because he was going to lose a lung, and right after that his best friend was killed, and he made the picture anyway, but while he was making the picture, he wrote a script that now Clint Eastwood and Shirley MacLaine are going to do—would you believe any horseshit

* Boetticher's book has not yet been published.

like that?" He said, "That's a pretty bad script." I said, "Well, it's true, isn't it?" He said, "O.K., I'll talk to you later." But that's what happened the last seven years. I thought, "That's the worst script I ever read. Nobody's gonna believe that one." But it's true.

I feel that I've never directed a picture in my life. I don't figure that I directed *Arruza*. I was there, and so were my cameras. In the other films, I had been experimenting. Now I'm ready to make some movies.

FILMOGRAPHY

Born July 29, 1918, in Chicago, Illinois. Boetticher was technical consultant on *Blood and Sand* (Rouben Mamoulian, 1941), assistant director on *Destroyer* (William A. Seiter, 1943), *The More the Merrier* (George Stevens, 1943), *The Desperadoes* (Charles Vidor, 1943), and *Cover Girl* (Charles Vidor, 1944).

One Mysterious Night—1944 (62 minutes)
Producer: Ted Richmond. *Script:* Paul Yawitz. *Photography:* Lionel O'Connell. *Cast:* Chester Morris, Janis Carter, Richard Lane, William Wright.

The Missing Juror—1944 (66 minutes)
Producer: Wallace MacDonald. *Script:* Charles O'Neal. *Photography:* Lionel O'Connell. *Cast:* Jim Bannon, Janis Carter, George Macready, Jean Stevens.

Youth on Trial—1944 (59 minutes)
Producer: Ted Richmond. *Script:* Michael Jacoby. *Photography:* George Meehan. *Cast:* Cora Sue Collins, David Reed, Eric Sinclair.

A Guy, a Gal, and a Pal—1945 (63 minutes)
Producer: Wallace MacDonald and Ross Hunter. *Script:* Monte Brice. *Photography:* Glan Gano. *Cast:* Ross Hunter, Lynn Merrick, Ted Donaldson, George Meeker.

Escape in the Fog—1945 (63 minutes)
Producer: Wallace MacDonald. *Script:* Aubrey Wisberg. *Photography:* George Meehan. *Cast:* Otto Kruger, Nina Foch, William Wright.

Assigned to Danger—1948 (66 minutes)
Producer: Eugene Ling. *Script:* Eugene Ling. *Photography:* Lionel O'Connell. *Cast:* Gene Raymond, Noreen Nash, Robert Bice, Martin Kosleck.

Behind Locked Doors—1948 (61 minutes)
Producer: Eugene Ling. *Script:* Malvin Wald and Eugene Ling. *Photography:* Robert Alton. *Cast:* Richard Carlson, Lucille Bremer, Douglas Fowley.

Black Midnight—1949 (66 minutes)
Producer: Lindsay Parsons. *Script:* Erna Lazarus and W. Scott Darling. *Photography:* William Sickner. *Cast:* Roddy McDowall, Damian O'Flynn, Lynn Thomas.

Wolf Hunters—1949 (70 minutes)
Producer: Lindsay Parsons and William Broidy. *Script:* W. Scott Darling. *Photography:* William Sickner. *Cast:* Kirby Grant, Jan Clayton, Edward Norris.

Killer Shark—1950 (76 minutes)
Producer: Lindsay Parsons. *Script:* Charles Lang. *Photography:* William Sickner. *Cast:* Roddy McDowall, Laurette Luez, Roland Winters, Edward Norris.

The Bullfighter and The Lady—1951 (85 minutes)
Producer: John Wayne. *Associate Producer:* Budd Boetticher. *Script:* James Edward Grant. *Photography:* Jack Draper. *Cast:* Robert Stack (Chuck Regan), Gilbert Roland (Manolo Estrada), Joy Page (Anita de la Vega), Katy Jurado (Chelo Estrada).

The Sword of D'Artagnan—1951 (50 minutes)
Producer: Hal Roach, Jr. *Script:* Roy Hamilton. *Photography:* Benjamin Kline. *Cast:* Robert Clarke, John Hubbard, Mel Archer, Keith Richards, Paul Cavanaugh, Marjorie Lord.

The Cimarron Kid—1951 (84 minutes)
Producer: Ted Richmond. *Script:* Louis Stevens. *Photography:* Charles P. Boyle. *Cast:* Audie Murphy, Beverly Tyler, Yvette Dugay, James Best, Noah Beery, Jr.

Bronco Buster—1952 (80 minutes)
Producer: Ted Richmond. *Script:* Horace McCoy and Lillie Hayward. *Photography:* Clifford Stine. *Cast:* John Lund, Scott Brady, Joyce

Holden, Chill Wills, Casey Tibbs.

Red Ball Express—1952 (84 minutes)
Producer: Aaron Rosenberg. *Script:* John Michael Hayes. *Photography:* Maury Gertsman. *Cast:* Jeff Chandler, Alex Nicol, Charles Drake, Judith Braun, Sidney Poitier.

Horizons West—1952 (81 minutes)
Producer: Albert J. Cohen. *Script:* Louis Stevens. *Photography:* Charles P. Boyle. *Cast:* Robert Ryan, Julia Adams, Rock Hudson, John McIntyre, Judith Braun, Raymond Burr, Dennis Weaver.

City Beneath the Sea—1953 (87 minutes)
Producer: Albert J. Cohen. *Script:* Jack Harvey and Ramon Romero. *Photography:* Charles P. Boyle. *Cast:* Robert Ryan, Mala Powers, Anthony Quinn, Susan Ball, Woody Strode.

Seminole—1953 (86 minutes)
Producer: Howard Christie. *Script:* Charles Peck, Jr. *Photography:* Russell Metty. *Cast:* Rock Hudson, Barbara Hale, Anthony Quinn, Richard Carlson, Hugh O'Brian, Lee Marvin, James Best.

The Man from the Alamo—1953 (79 minutes)
Producer: Aaron Rosenberg. *Script:* Steve Fischer and D. D. Beauchamp. *Photography:* Russell Metty. *Cast:* Glenn Ford, Julia Adams, Chill Wills, Hugh O'Brian, Victor Jory.

Wings of the Hawk—1953 (80 minutes)
Producer: Aaron Rosenberg. *Script:* James E. Moser. *Photography:* Clifford Stine. *Cast:* Van Heflin, Julia Adams, Abbe Lane, George Dolenz, Pedro Gonzales-Gonzales.

East of Sumatra—1953 (82 minutes)
Producer: Albert J. Cohen. *Script:* Frank Gill, Jr. *Photography:* Clifford Stine. *Cast:* Jeff Chandler, Marilyn Maxwell, Anthony Quinn, Susan Ball, Jay C. Flippen, "Scat Man" Cruwthers.

The Magnificent Matador—1955 (94 minutes)
Producer: Edward L. Alperson. *Script:* Charles Lang. *Photography:* Lucien Ballard. *Cast:* Anthony Quinn, Maureen O'Hara, Manuel Rojas,

Richard Denning, Thomas Gomez, Lola Albright.

The Killer Is Loose—1955 (73 minutes)
Producer: Robert L. Jacks. *Script:* Harold Medford. *Photography:* Lucien Ballard. *Cast:* Joseph Cotten, Rhonda Fleming, Wendell Corey, Alan Hale, Jr., Michael Pate.

Seven Men from Now—1956 (78 minutes)
Producer: Andrew V. McLaglen and Robert E. Morrison. *Script:* Burt Kennedy. *Photography:* William H. Clothier. *Cast:* Randolph Scott (Ben Stride), Gail Russell (Anne Greer), Lee Marvin (Masters), Walter Reed (John Greer).

The Tall T—1957 (78 minutes)
Producer: Harry Joe Brown. *Script:* Burt Kennedy. *Photography:* Charles Lawton, Jr. *Cast:* Randolph Scott (Pat Brennan), Maureen O'Sullivan (Doretta Mims), Richard Boone (Frank Usher), Arthur Hunnicutt (Ed Rintoon), Skip Homeier (Billy Jack), Henry Silva (Chink).

Decision at Sundown—1957 (77 minutes)
Producer: Harry Joe Brown. *Script:* Charles Lang, Jr. *Photography:* Burnett Guffey. *Cast:* Randolph Scott (Bart Allison), John Carroll (Tate Kimborough), Karen Steele (Lucy Summerton), Valerie French (Ruby James), Noah Beery, Jr. (Sam), John Archer (Doc Storrow), Andrew Duggan (Swede Hanson).

Buchanan Rides Alone—1958 (78 minutes)
Producer: Harry Joe Brown. *Script:* Charles Lang, Jr. *Photography:* Lucien Ballard. *Cast:* Randolph Scott (Buchanan), Craig Stevens (Carbo), Barry Kelly (Lew Agry), Tol Avery (Simon Agry), Peter Whitney (Amos Agry), Manuel Rojas (Juan de la Vega).

Ride Lonesome—1959 (73 minutes)
Producer: Budd Boetticher. *Script:* Burt Kennedy. *Photography:* Charles Lawton, Jr. *Cast:* Randolph Scott (Ben Brigade), Karen Steele (Carrie), Pernell Roberts (Sam Boone), James Coburn (Wid), Lee Van Cleef (Frank), James Best (Billy John).

Westbound—1959 (72 minutes)

Producer: Henry Blanke. *Script:* Berne Giler. *Photography:* J. Peverell Marley. *Cast:* Randolph Scott (John Hayes), Karen Steele (Jeannie Miller), Virginia Mayo (Norma Putnam), Andrew Duggan (Clay Putnam), Michael Dante (Rod Miller), Michael Pate (Mace).

Comanche Station—1960 (73 minutes)

Producer: Budd Boetticher. *Script:* Burt Kennedy. *Photography:* Charles Lawton, Jr. *Cast:* Randolph Scott (Jefferson Cody), Nancy Gates (Mrs. Lowe), Claude Akins (Ben Lane), Skip Homeier (Frank), Richard Rust (Dobie).

The Rise and Fall of Legs Diamond—1960 (101 minutes)

Producer: Milton Sperling. *Script:* Joseph Landon. *Photography:* Lucien Ballard. *Cast:* Ray Danton (Jack "Legs" Diamond), Karen Steele (Alice Diamond), Elaine Stewart (Monica), Jesse White (Leo Bremer), Robert Lowery (Arnold Rothstein), Warren Oates (Eddie Diamond), Joseph Ruskin (Matt Moren).

Arruza—1969 (90 minutes)

Producer: Budd Boetticher. *Script:* Budd Boetticher. *Photography:* Carlos Caravajal. *Cast:* Carlos Arruza, Mari Arruza.

A Time for Dying—1969 (75 minutes)

Producer: Audie Murphy. *Script:* Budd Boetticher. *Photography:* Lucien Ballard. *Cast:* Anne Randall, Richard Lapp, Bob Brandon, Victor Jory, Terry Murphy.

When There's Sumpthin' to Do—1969 (70 minutes)

Producer: Audie Murphy. *Script:* Budd Boetticher. *Cast:* Audie Murphy, Gaston Santos, Bob Random.

Peter Bogdanovich

INTRODUCTION

Peter Bogdanovich's first film, *Targets,* deals with a young, average, middle-class American male who, one day, murders his wife and family, takes pot-shots at rapidly moving cars on a freeway, then hides behind the screen of a drive-in theater and shoots at a few dozen more people. When he finally is caught, his last line is "Hardly ever missed, did I?" This tale of modern horror is paralleled by a sub-plot involving Boris Karloff as an aging monster-movie star who finds himself more laughed at as a camp hero than feared as a symbol of Gothic horror. The two plots progress until there is a final, inevitable confrontation between Karloff and the boy at the drive-in.

The plot, along with the original advertising campaign for the film ("Why Gun Control?"), might lead the casual observer to expect

another straight social-problem film—"Right Out of the Shadows of Today's Headlines!," as they used to say. However, the social aspects of *Targets* are of secondary importance to the fact that the film marks the debut of the first American film critic to go into the Hollywood system as a director.

At one point in the film, Byron Orlok (Karloff) and Sammy Michaels (played by Bogdanovich), a young director intent on resurrecting the elegance of past action-horror films, sit down and watch a movie on television. The audience is then treated to a brief clip from *The Criminal Code,* made in 1931 by one of Bogdanovich's favorite directors, Howard Hawks. This moment marks what is probably the first full-fledged cinematic "quote" in American cinema. In this sense, the invocation of Hawks differs from, for example, the sequence from *Queen Kelly* in Wilder's *Sunset Boulevard* or from the excerpt from *Bad and the Beautiful* in Minnelli's *Two Weeks in Another Town,* which are used more for purposes of nostalgic-historical and personal-Pirandellian reminiscence, respectively, than for indicating critical intelligence.

Bogdanovich is able to integrate this reference into the context of *Targets* to the extent that it neither belies an abysmal gap between example and model (as did the sequence from *Picnic on the Grass* in Agnes Varda's *Le Bonheur*), nor becomes merely an esoteric allusion (such as the reference to *Viaggio en Italia* in Godard's *Contempt*). The *Criminal Code* reference ties into the plot of *Targets,* since the earlier film marked the first major appearance of Karloff in a motion picture. More important, the film clip (which portrays a steadily rising crescendo of pure noise during a prison riot) parallels the spasmodic bursts of music which emanated from the boy's car radio earlier in the film, and thus reinforces the film's central tension between the simple richness of the past and the complex sterility of the modern world—even our ears respond differently to the two periods. The melodramatic intensity of Hawks' scene (which is frustratingly cut off by a commercial) also prepares us for the film's climax in which melodrama is affirmed and social reality sacked. Bogdanovich transcends pretension and in-joke, and he integrates a valid reference into an American film for the first time. A localized victory, perhaps, but an important one in a period of film history when critical self-consciousness is becoming more and more inevitable.

In the scene, the young director comments, "He [Hawks] sure knows how to tell a story." Storytelling is a dominant trait in Bogdanovich's own visual style and selection of theme. Bogdanovich makes no attempt in *Targets* to explain the gruesome situation. Instead, he concentrates on *showing* the murders and the corpses in order to make the audience

observe and feel the terror he portrays. This reliance on the simple and
direct machinery of the action genre co-exists with the critical sensibility
in the film. The juxtaposition of these two elements at times creates an
extraordinary ambivalence (as in the climax of the film, which suspends
the viewer between contradictory desires to emotionalize as well as
intellectualize the moment) which indicates one of the first potentially
productive marriages between the "new" criticism and the traditional
style of film-making.

Some of the plot constructions and cutting in *Targets,* together with
surface echoes of *North by Northwest, Strangers on a Train,* and *Psycho,*
have caused critics to label the film "Hitchcockian" (a catch-all label
which seems to be applied to any film involving murder and suspense
these days). This interpretation is based mainly on the freeway murder
scenes, which have been said to convey therapeutic audience identification in the manner of The Master. The parallel only partially holds up.
In *Targets* the feeling inspired by glimpses through the telescopic mount
and huge close-ups of the boy's hands and rifle seems to be mostly one

of a detached, clinical admiration for the precise mechanics of lining up
the sights and pulling the trigger, rather than the tremendous emotional-
moral involvement and therapeutic shock which is registered by an anal-
ogous shot of Raymond Burr *directly* confronting the audience through
James Stewart's field-glasses in *Rear Window.* Rather than involving us
in an irresistible fascination with guilt and psychological darkness, as
Hitchcock does, Bogdanovich fashions his moral statement by utilizing

our interest in observing a job well done. Throughout *Targets* neither the action nor the images indicate that Bogdanovich is primarily interested in the psychological depth which films like *Vertigo* and *Psycho* convey.

Even though *Targets* is closer to Hitchcock than are *The Bride Wore Black, Rosemary's Baby, Wait Until Dark,* and other such pallid imitations, Bogdanovich's visual style seems much more influenced by Hawks? The flat visual surfaces of the shots in *Targets* reflect the equal

geometric dispersion of the elements in one of Hawks' classical compositions, which unite foreground and background, action and setting, with equal depth into a single spatial whole. In each case, the unification of the elements of the shot into a single texture is used to express a direct, continuous tension between these elements, particularly characters and environment.

The difference in the visual styles of Hawks and Bogdanovich is one of emphasis, as well as depth and experience. In Hawks, the outer environment is abstract (either a nihilistic, black void that surrounds the characters in, for example, *Only Angels Have Wings* and *To Have and Have Not,* or the chaotic patterns of the large-scale action—the airplane battles in *The Dawn Patrol* and the racing scenes in *Red Line 7000*), and the characters are concrete. In *Targets,* on the other hand, the environ-

ment is concrete (The Plastic Society), and the characters are abstract (a collection of types and surfaces). In other words, the dominant details in *Targets* are realized not in the characterizations but in the settings. Many of the characters slip the mind, but we remember the drive-in, the suburban homes, the projection room, the shooting range, the oil tanks. Bogdanovich is interested in his characters' behavioral patterns as an outgrowth of their society, while Hawks follows his characters' response to (and against) their surroundings, which takes the form of moral codes and desperate ethics. Accordingly, Bogdanovich's compositions lack the tension of Hawks'. In this way, Bogdanovich is able to present his social angle in cinematic rather than sociological terms. Thus, of necessity, he sacrifices some of Hawks' universality—settings (or social milieu) date more easily than characters.

As a critic, Bogdanovich is one of the few American writers who try to approach films and directors on their terms. His books on John Ford and Fritz Lang are more presentations of these men's personalities than academic analyses of their social and political concerns. Bogdanovich's writing reflects the belief that more can be learned by directly observing the stylistic and thematic interplay between a director's personality and his films than by applying an abstract set of aesthetic principles concerning "filmic space," "filmic time," "the film experience," "camera vision," etc. The direct experiential aspects of film, too often submerged today in a morass of generalities, inform and intensify Bogdanovich's writing as well as his film-making.

The following interview was conducted at Mr. Bogdanovich's home in Van Nuys, California, in November 1968.

M.R.

INTERVIEW

Bogdanovich: I always considered myself a director who was making a living writing about pictures, not the other way around. In other words, I had always wanted to direct films, even when I didn't know it. The writing was something I never really cared much about.

I was on the stage first. We've all sinned! I directed plays in New York. The first thing I did was *The Big Knife* by Clifford Odets. I directed and co-produced it off-Broadway in 1959–60. It was a successful production critically, but it didn't last too long—a couple of months. I had never directed anything before that except a scene from *The Big Knife* for one of Stella Adler's acting classes. From the time I was fifteen, I studied acting with Stella. I had also done some acting with the American and the New York Shakespeare Festivals.

Then I directed a season of summer theater in Phoenicia, New York, in 1961. I did four plays, among them Agatha Christie's *Ten Little Indians,* which was the best thing I ever did. I did *Ten Little Indians* à la Hawks or Welles—it was the fastest production you've ever seen. Every line overlapped with another. You know Agatha Christie—it was all exposition, dull as hell. The first act was forty-six pages, and it played in twenty-six minutes. The whole thing was just a set-up for a murder. I tried for a great effect in the last act. I killed every light in the theater, including the exit lights. It was absolutely black. The audience started to get screaming mad. Suddenly you heard this rustling noise on the stage, then a gunshot. Bang! You saw the actors for just one second, like a one-frame cut. It was very exciting.

In those years, I began to write a lot about movies. I wrote monographs for the Museum of Modern Art on Orson Welles in 1961, on Howard Hawks in 1962, and on Alfred Hitchcock in 1963. I was asked to do these because I had written some program notes for the New Yorker Theater [a New York movie house]. I helped Dan Talbot, the owner, program some films in the theater's early months. That's where I got to know who Hawks was. We booked a lot of pictures just so I could see them. In 1962, I started to write for *Esquire.* I did pieces on Jerry Lewis, Jimmy Stewart, John Ford, Humphrey Bogart, and others.

q. Your film criticism is really different from most of that being written in this country. How did you develop your ideas? Was it through seeing films, or were there outside influences like *Cahiers du Cinema* and Andrew Sarris? Did you start out, like most of us, in the art-house cycle of Bergman, Fellini, Kurosawa?

a. The main influences were Andrew Sarris and Eugene Archer. Archer was the fourth-string critic for the *New York Times,* and he was brilliant. He influenced a lot of Sarris' opinions. He and Sarris opened my eyes to films. They got me to see films like *Land of the Pharaohs* [Howard Hawks, 1955] and *Fort Apache* [John Ford, 1948]. I was stupid about certain things. I didn't like *Psycho* at the time. I thought it was brilliant but immoral, or something idiotic like that. I remember sitting over coffee one night, and they explained to me why *Psycho* was a great film. They had a big influence on me for about two years, opening things up. But I was ready for that, because I had already gone through my art-film cycle. I was past all that.

Truthfully, my best days as a film-goer were around the time I was ten. My taste was purest then. My favorite films were *Red River* [Hawks, 1948] and *She Wore a Yellow Ribbon* [Ford, 1949]. I saw the first about five times and the second about ten times. Then, as I grew older, I was influenced by critics, as we all are, and my taste went bad. I used to sit in the Thalia [a New York art-house] and look at all those boring foreign films. My taste was really formed when I booked all those films at the New Yorker. We had a series called "The Forgotten Film," and in the first two weeks we had about ten Hawks pictures. That was a revelation to me. You see, I really always loved Hawks. When *Rio*

Bravo came out, I loved it, but I didn't know about Hawks. Then I said, "Wait a minute! He did *Red River!*" I put it all together. I had liked all his films, but I hadn't known who he was.

I think too many critics write about a movie as though it exists alone in time. This is crazy. You have to take every movie not only in the perspective of the other films of that director, but also in the whole context of film history—which isn't very long, so I don't know why it isn't done. The worst thing we have in film writing is a lack of film scholarship and the fact that the first thirty years are virtually lost.

A whole school of critics think they like movies, but they don't. They think it's all very nice to like films—within limits. You can't have a passion for them, because after all, it's still a bit juvenile to sit in a movie theater for six hours. Something's not quite right about it. However, people who read books for hours are eggheads, geniuses. It's really a kind of Victorian anti-movie theory.

After my off-Broadway production of *Once in a Lifetime* flopped in 1964, Frank Tashlin [the film director] came to see us. I was depressed. He said, "What are you going to do now?" I said, "I don't know." He said, "What do you want to do?" I said, "I want to make pictures." He said, "Then what are you doing in New York? If you want to make pictures, come to the West Coast. That's where they're made."

He planted the idea in my head. Three months later my wife, Polly, and I moved out here with the expressed purpose of continuing to write and hopefully to make a movie. It never occurred to me that I'd be directing a film in less than two years. To sum up, I always wanted to direct, but I must say that being a critic led me into it. My first job on any picture was a direct result of my having written, and that was with Roger Corman.

In 1965, I went to a screening of *Bay of Angels*. Sitting behind me were Roger Corman and a mutual acquaintance. He introduced me to Roger, who had heard of me through my *Esquire* articles. Roger called me a couple of days later and said, "You're a writer. Wouldn't you like to write for pictures?" "Sure, I'd love to." He said, "I'm looking for something along the lines of *Lawrence of Arabia* or *Bridge on the River Kwai.*" I said, "Oh! Well, that's not too difficult!" So Polly and I started to work on a story about World War II.

In January 1966 Roger called me again and said, "I'm going to start a picture called *The Wild Angels*. Would you like to work on it?" I said, "Sure. What do you want me to do?" He said, "I don't know. Just be around." I asked him how long it would take. He said six weeks. So I went to work for Roger. *The Wild Angels* was quite an odyssey, it stretched out to twenty-two weeks.

First I had to find locations for the picture. Then, about ten days before the start of shooting, believe it or not, the script came in. I read it, and it was terrible. It had all these ridiculous sequences like: horse's point of view, cut to frog, motorcycles, cut to frog's point of view as the motorcycles go by. I said to Roger, "This is a Disney picture!" Roger said, "I know. What am I going to do?" I said, "Why don't you rewrite it?" He said, "Oh, no. I don't have time." Jumping in, opportunistic bastard that I am, I said, "I'll do some work on it." He said, "Well . . . O.K."

I rewrote about eighty per cent of the script, although a lot of the dialogue was changed on the set. The actors wouldn't pay any attention to it. They each added about forty "man" 's to every line. In a way that helped, because the actors had spent some time with the Hell's Angels and knew their dialect. Afterwards, somebody called me up and said, "Didn't you work on the script for that picture?" I said, "Yes. How did you know?" You see, I didn't receive any official credit for the screenplay. He said, "Well, it has a line that's right out of *Rio Bravo!*" When Peter Fonda and the others go into a garage to get back The Loser's

stolen bike, he says, "One of you guys here stole a bike." The other guy says, "Nobody here stole nothin'." Fonda says, "I'll *remember* you said that." He didn't say it quite as well as John Wayne did.

Anyway, we started to shoot. We fell behind schedule very quickly, because the motorcycles gave us problems. Roger kept throwing sequences out and saying, "I can't do this. The second unit will do it." I said, "There *is* no second unit." He said, "I know, I know!" I said, "Well, I'd love to do it." So I shot all the second-unit stuff: backgrounds for the main title, all the sequences of Fonda riding through L.A. I also shot the entire chase on the mountain between Loser and the cop. I was trying to do the chase in *High Sierra* [Raoul Walsh, 1941], and I failed. I tried to repeat that chase in *Targets,* when the cop is chasing the boy.

I shot another scene that I thought was very funny. It's at night, when Peter Fonda comes back to his house. He sees the police are there. Depressed, he goes back to his motorcycle and starts it up. Roger had said, "We don't have any scenes where we show Fonda's attachment to his motorcycle." This came about because one of the real Angels said to Roger, "You don't show how we dig our bikes, man." So Roger said, "Let's have a scene where he's loving his bike." Being very literal, I said, "Let's show him screwing it!" So we did. Later, the editor said, "We don't have any music for this scene." I said, "Why don't you put in the sound of a couple of cats screwing?" I was just joking. He said, "That's a good idea!" They got a couple of cats, and I don't know what they did to them, but they got the sound.

After I shot for two or three weeks with different units, I got to cut the footage, because the editor was tired and had so much else to do. Some kid showed me the mechanics, and then I did most of it myself with a Moviola in my living room. I never had so much fun. I never enjoyed anything so much as physically cutting the film, which I also did on *Targets.*

The Wild Angels was eventually finished. My voice is in it, and I even run through it. If you look carefully, you can see me getting beat up by the Hell's Angels, who were used as extras. You see, I was always with Roger, and they hated Roger, so they hated me, too. During the final fight scene, we needed more extras, so Roger said to me, "Run in

there!" Well, they just tried to kill me—they really did. I fell to the ground, and they murdered me.

Anyway, when the picture was finished, I had received, in twenty-two weeks, a paid course on just about everything you could do in a picture: scouting locations, writing script, directing, getting laundry, acting, cutting, doing sound work. I learned a hell of a lot. That was 1966.

The picture turned out to be a big hit. Roger called me and said, "Thank you, but rather than thanking you, I'd like to ask you if you would want to direct a picture." I said, "Of course. What do you want me to do?" He said, "Look, Boris Karloff made a picture with me called *The Terror* and part of the deal is he still owes me two days. Here's what I want you to do: Shoot with Karloff for two days. Get about twenty minutes of footage. Then take about twenty minutes of Karloff out of *The Terror*. Then shoot another forty minutes with some other actors, put it all together, and I'll have a new Karloff picture!"

I'm skipping one thing that was also part of the deal. Roger had bought a Russian picture called *Storm Clouds of Venus* or something like that. Unbelievably bad film. Roger said, "I've got a deal with AIP

[American International Pictures]. They'll buy this picture, but they want some girls in it. Just shoot for five days, and stick some girls in. Then you can do the Karloff picture. It'll all be one package deal." Well, putting those women in that goddamned picture dragged on for months. It was the worst thing I've ever had to do.

Finally, I thought of a way of putting girls in: they'd be "gill-women" on Venus. Mamie Van Doren was the lead girl. The picture is now called *Voyage to the Planet of Prehistoric Women,* but I made it as *Gill-Women of Venus:* you see how art is corrupted. The idea was that these guys come to Venus. Since the original actors were Russian, we couldn't intermingle the two parts. I got the idea of showing the women looking at the men, but the men never see *them.* It was a damn good idea.

In the Russian picture, the men kill a pterodactyl. So I made it the god of the gill-women. They worship a statue of a pterodactyl. Since the men killed one, the women now want to kill the men. There was a rain sequence in the original. So the women call upon the god, and the rains fall—they try to drown the men. The original had a volcano sequence. So I have the women try to kill the men with the volcano. It doesn't kill them, but it makes them leave the planet.

In the Russian picture, the men have this big, wonderful robot who can do everything. In the volcano sequence, the only thing that gets hurt is the robot. It floats away in the lava. So I wrote in that the girls find the robot encrusted with lava. For $300, we faked a robot and encrusted it with lava. My ending was that when the men fly away, the girls realize that these guys were stronger than their god. So they knock down the pterodactyl and put up the robot. That's their new god. The sad thing is that these guys could have banged the beautiful gill-women if they had only stuck around.

It was so exhausting, much more than anything on *Targets*. Almost killed me. It went on and on. Finally, I wrote this narration which is told by one of the guys on the Russian ship. At the end of the film, the Russians find this little stone which has a sculpture of one of the women on it. But it's too late, and they blast off anyway. The narration comes on: "I know she's there. Maybe some day I'll find her. Maybe I'll die trying." Which is a switch on the last line of *The Lady from Shanghai* [Orson Welles, 1948]!

Anyway, it was an awful picture with nothing to commend it except some inside jokes and some nice shots. If I had to do it again today, I'd have the women fighting each other, ripping each other's cockleshells off (they wore shells over their breasts). I'd make it sexy. But now, as you can tell, it's just lyrical and simply awful. This took up so much time that I couldn't get to the Karloff picture. I had worked on *Gill-Women* until October 1966.

The evolution of *Targets* is quite interesting, because we started out by having Karloff as a heavy, a strangler. Then, I had an idea for a joke. The only fairly good sequence in *The Terror* was the flood. It lasted twenty minutes. I was going to cut it down to two minutes and open the picture with it. "The End" comes on the screen. We cut to the inside of a projection room. Lights come on. Sitting in the front row is Boris Karloff. Next to him is Roger Corman. Boris turns to him and says, "Well, Roger, it's really frightful, isn't it?" From that came an idea. I said, "Hey, wait a minute. Karloff is an actor! Then the footage is of him as an actor, and I don't have to use it as the story." Believe it or not, that little thing made all the difference in the world. Then I could pawn off the *Terror* footage; I didn't have to take credit for it.

So, first Karloff was the heavy. Now he's an actor. He's been playing horror-monster parts all his life, and he hates it. What he really wants to do is to be Cary Grant. So he goes into his room in the daytime (I like murder in the daytime), he pushes a secret button, and there's his dressing room. He puts on a handsome mask, and he goes out and strangles women in supermarkets. I wanted that, because the floor of a supermarket is great for dollying. You know, you have this shot of a murder, and you pan up, and a sign says, "PEAS REDUCED THIS WEEK." This shows you the kinds of ideas you can have when you're desperate.

But we were still working under the theory that Karloff would be the heavy. Finally, Polly and I decided that was a stupid idea. What were we going to do? Make another picture like *The Gill-Women*? Or

would we do something good? Polly said that we should have a modern killer. We both decided that the most modern, terrifying murderer— *modern horror*—was the sniper in Texas.

We started to develop a story about Karloff as an actor and a boy like that sniper. Originally, the two met early in the picture, and they knew each other. As the script developed, we thought more and more that they shouldn't meet. I took the treatment to Sam Fuller and asked him for his views on it. Sam had some great ideas and helped us a lot with the construction of the story. I wrote the script based on that treatment. Roger liked it, and we cast it. Roger paid for the whole picture. It's all his money. $130,000.

q.   What about this "Why Gun Control?" angle that was used in the film's publicity and was tacked on to the film as a prologue? How

socially conscious did you intend the film to be?

a. I didn't at all. The gun control pitch came about because Senator Kennedy was shot after Paramount bought the film. As you know, everybody felt weird about censorship and violence. Paramount thought the gun control notion would be a respectable way of selling the picture. I felt that it wouldn't be good for the picture financially, because message pictures are usually box-office poison. But frankly, if they hadn't put that on, I don't think the picture would have been released this year. Everybody was scared.

The gun control angle helped us with some critics. It also hurt us with several critics who started to look for a message or a statement about Why He Did It. We didn't tell why he did it. We never wanted to. The ad said, "This Picture Sheds a Little Light on a Dark Topic." I don't think we shed much light on it. I wasn't trying to shed light on it. I just wanted to *show* the thing. In fact, the most horrifying thing about these murders is that there doesn't seem to be any reason commensurate with the size of the crime. So I didn't have any socially conscious motivations at all. By the way, that prologue has now been taken off the picture.

q. Were you satisfied with the narrative structure of *Targets*—telling two stories at once?

a. It was very tough to do. While we were making it the nagging worry was: would it work to tell the two stories so independently of each other? I always thought it would because audiences have seen enough movies so that they would just *know* the two of them would meet. Just because he's Boris Karloff and the boy is the other star of the picture. Whether they knew it or not, they would feel it. It's a sort of unspoken quality of suspense.

But it's not easy to tell a story like that. On the one hand, you're worried about whether the audience can jump from one thing to another. On the other hand, that's good, because if a scene gets dull, you can cut away to the other story without an excuse. I tried very much not to cut on moves or subject matter the way Brooks did in *In Cold Blood*. I did it once, when I panned from Karloff to a table and then cut to an identical pan to the boy. If I had to do it again, I'd cut the pan. It's too self-conscious.

q. Although you would like to avoid self-consciousness, there seem to be many rather obvious "quotes" in the film. For example, when the boy is arranging the bodies of his family, it reminded me of Anthony Perkins cleaning up after the murder of Janet Leigh in *Psycho*. Also, when the boy drops his guns and is reaching for them, that reminded me of Robert Walker going after the lighter in *Strangers on a Train*.

a. The *Psycho* one wasn't conscious. Although the cleanliness idea was the same, it's not really done in the same way. Perkins is much more thorough than my boy. The sequence in *Psycho* is phenomenally brilliant, and I don't particularly like the scene in *Targets*. It came out of some-

thing that the Whitman boy really did in Texas. He put his wife and mother to bed after he killed them. I thought it was a chilling touch, so I used it in the film. He buried them, so to speak. The cleaning-up was just carrying that out. If I had thought of *Psycho,* the sequence might have been a little better.

The *Strangers* reference wasn't conscious either. When I saw the footage, I realized what I had done, but not while I was shooting. The most fascinating thing is that it was all subconscious. Of course, *all* of

that drive-in sequence is *Strangers:* timing, dusk, music. I didn't know that at the time. About three months later, I saw *Strangers* again and said, "Jesus Christ! Look at this!" However, I made some references consciously. For example, there's a shot from the top of the tank as the boy runs away—I pan from the stuff he left behind over to him running. That's from *North by Northwest,* when Cary Grant runs out of the U.N.—a shot I've always loved.

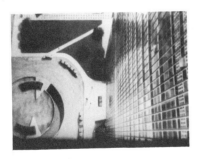 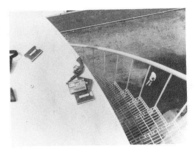

   q.   What do you think the relevance of these cinematic quotes is? Do you think they're a valid form of self-expression?

   a.   Just as much as in any other art. Novelists will quote and even imitate other writers for a definite purpose. I think most novelists begin by consciously imitating others to get a certain effect, not as parody or homage, but because the other writers "do it good," and you know it'll be good if you do it their way.

   Sometimes you're criticized for stealing. On the contrary, I think it's admirable, because nothing's original anymore. It's all been done. They were doing it in the silent days—all this split-screen junk and fast cutting. I just interviewed Allan Dwan, and he said that he had done it way back when he was making films in the 1920's. He said, "That's the kind of stuff we threw away when we grew up."

One of my pleasures in making films is sometimes to reproduce shots that I've seen and loved. For example, I love one of the corniest shots ever done. You see it in any Johnny Mack Brown Western: the guy rides by, and you pan back to see the people who are chasing him. I just love that shot, so I used it in the chase in *Targets*. It's a good piece of grammar, a good sentence. It says, "Here he goes; now let's see how far back they are." It's a continuous movement, and the audience knows that nothing's been manipulated, that it's real. I don't think it's possible for anyone who's starting to make films today not to be influenced by what's gone before. Ford, Hawks, Dwan, and these other directors have already done everything, and *they* were all influenced by Griffith. Unless you're some sort of primitive talent, you have to know the history of what came before to be any good.

Also, I think that in my film, there's a criticism of other films. When I make a picture, I'm criticizing other pictures by doing something that is opposed to the way others are doing it. Sternberg once said that *The Salvation Hunters* was a criticism of other pictures. They said, "What do you mean?" He said, "All the others were fast, and mine was slow." Well, *Targets* is a criticism of other pictures in a way, too, because I don't split the screen, I don't have any arty cutting or arty shots, and I don't move the camera for no reason at all. It's a very Jesuit film—self-denying. I didn't indulge myself at all. I was telling a thriller, and I didn't want to indulge in any ego shots. So the film is a criticism of a self-conscious style.

To give you an example, there's a shot in *Targets* of the boy going toward the tanks. He opens a chain-link gate, and the camera dollies with him, with the fence in the foreground. Behind him are all kinds of religious floats that were kept in storage and brought out during Christmas and Easter. Of course, the temptation was very great to shoot from the other side. You'd see crosses in the foreground—sort of an Aldrich shot, or Aldrich doing Welles. I love Welles, but I didn't want to do that, because everybody's doing it. I purposely said, "No. Keep it in the background. Don't get fancy." I didn't want everybody to nudge one another and say, "Oh! He's making a religious point." I just wanted to show the boy going to the tanks.

I try to avoid as much of that as possible. Whenever I'm tempted, I try not to. I've been thinking of doing an absolutely insane baroque movie next, but I probably won't, because I prefer the simplicity of Hawks, Walsh, Ford, and even Hitchcock. Hitchcock doesn't have any arty shots. They may be odd, but they're always done for an emotional, not an artistic, effect—like the cut to the high angle in *The Man Who Knew Too Much* when Stewart hears that his son has been kidnapped. It's got to hit you in an emotional way.

q.   One critic said that *Targets* was the logical movie for a film critic to make. He was referring to your cinematic quotes. But he expressed bitterness and resentment.

a.   Yes, most American film critics resent any sense of passion for movies. For example one critic commented on the various color patterns in *Targets* and the sterility of the boy's house. He said that he doubted I had intended it. Well, this is the biggest insult of all. That was all planned in the film. It's patronizing. It's like saying, "A movie director can't think those big thoughts."

I wrote a piece for *New York* magazine about these forty educators in Santa Barbara who saw *Targets*. They attacked me for making a commercial picture, a sell-out. Sell-out! Hah! I'd hate to tell you what I got paid for *Targets*. It's funny, because I'm usually defending other directors who are accused of selling out, like Siegel, Ford, Walsh. The accusers are the same kind of people who say, "Yes, Hitchcock's really talented. It's a pity he doesn't make anything good. Those awful stories— why doesn't he make something important?" These are the people who listen to films; they don't watch them. They're concerned with the literary content and nothing beyond it.

q.   The visual style of *Targets* struck me as being very planar,

almost two-dimensional. It seemed to create a flat sense of space around the characters.

    a. We wanted a contrast between Karloff's world and the boy's world, so we were careful with the color control. The Karloff sequences were all brown, gold, yellow—warm colors. The boy's sequences were green, blue, white—cold colors. I wanted to make the boy's home, as much as possible, like the homes here in the San Fernando Valley. The houses really are that way—blank walls. We made it even more bare.

We wanted a kind of sterility. What Norman Mailer calls "The Plastic Society." I was very much influenced by Mailer's essays on architecture, particularly *Cannibals and Christians,* in the whole concept of the boy's life. Rather than give a reason for the murders, I just wanted to convey that the boy is an outgrowth of this kind of society. In fact, at one point I wanted to shoot the film during Christmas out here, because the street decorations in L.A. are not to be believed. The plastic angels on Van Nuys Boulevard are just marvelous. Some day, I will shoot a horror story during Christmas in L.A.

    q.   What about this two-dimensional aspect?

    a.   It comes from not wanting to be decorative. I wanted a kind of simplicity. I tried to get more shadows and depth into the Karloff scenes, but I don't think it worked that well. I think the boy's scenes are much more successful. If I could reshoot the film I'd do many things differently.

    q.   I think a tension between sophistication and your desire for simplicity is very apparent in *Targets*. It gives the film an unusual sense of depth at certain points—for example, in the scene where Karloff comes toward the boy at the foot of the movie screen, and the boy shoots first

at Karloff's image on the screen and then at the real Karloff. In one sense, this scene has sophisticated connotations: illusion and reality, schizophrenia, and all that. In another sense, though, it's the simplest and most innocent story in the world: the old story of the cowboy in the early 1900's who shot at the villain on the screen when he saw a movie for the first time.

a.   You're right. I was more worried about that scene than anything else in the picture. I thought that we stood the chance of getting laughed out of the theater. The idea was Sam Fuller's. Sam has a simpler, more basic approach to a story than I do. At first, I found the scene hard to believe in. Then I embraced it as a marvelous kind of melodramatic thing.

Of course, the whole drive-in scene is illusion-reality. The boy shooting through the screen is like reality breaking through illusion. Originally I wanted to have a shot of the whole drive-in from above the candy stand. Slowly the camera would start moving in toward the screen. It goes all the way in, and then you see the gun poking through the screen. We couldn't do it, because it was too complicated. What you saw was a compromise; it was done with a cut. But the idea was the same: looking at an illusion and out of it comes this harsh reality.

I think that what you saw is that I tried to intellectualize the moment for myself. I had to say, "Now, what am I doing here?" I thought it was hokey and melodramatic, but also very theatrical and effective. So, all through the picture, with the plot, I tried to prepare for that moment. For that reason, I think it works.

One critic made an interesting point. He said that he thought the ending was not meant to be realistic. He thought that it was my way of saying that art would triumph over reality. Although I really didn't have that in mind, I thought it was a very nice way of reading the ending. I think Karloff wins in the picture because I wanted him to.

q.   Yes, but do you have any particular feelings about this tension?

a.   Well, I think that's something you've spotted in me. I have an intellectual background. My father is an artist. On the other hand, I'm attracted to the less intellectual aspects of things. I try to fight against that. I respond emotionally—and I suppose intellectually, too—to Hawks, Walsh, Hitchcock. I have that duality, that tension in me. If it comes through in the picture, that's good, because it's part of me.

You see, a Walsh picture like *High Sierra* has much more than most people see. It's intuitive—*intelligent* rather than intellectual. I like to see that intuitive intelligence at work. With the exception of Welles, who is, I think, more consciously intellectual, I like the intuitive directors better —Ford, Walsh, Hawks. I know I work better when I do things intuitively. For instance, I thought some of the best stuff in *Targets* was the boy's characterization. I don't know how he behaved in real life, but I followed my emotions. It's been successful; audiences are chilled by that.

Also, I must say I'm attracted to the kind of action film that I would like to make and am *going* to make. I think sequences in *Targets* work on an action level. However, I don't think I could make a pure action film, unfortunately. I probably don't have the purity to do it.

So, I'm fighting against the intellectual part of my own nature, I guess. For example, I think the Karloff sequences, which are intellectual, are the weakest things in the picture. The best sequences are the drive-in, the freeway shooting, and the chase. I get the biggest kick out of seeing them with an audience and feeling the silence when they're really gripped. I watched the film with my agent in a projection room, and after it was over, I heard him let go of his breath. That was the biggest kick I got— the kind of emotional involvement I want.

That's why I think Hitchcock is so good. He has that ability to really manipulate an audience. It's just like making people laugh. But I get more satisfaction out of suspense, because it's harder to do. People will laugh at a lot of things: look at all the TV shows. To make somebody really nervous is very difficult.

People say, "Oh, Hitchcock. The Master of Suspense. Big deal." Well, wait a minute. That's not so easy to do. Film is the most emotional medium in the world. That's why this whole literary approach, publishing scripts and so on, is so ridiculous. Film affects you. It has nothing to do with anything else. If you're able to stop and think about a movie, which you can't do if it's done well, then it's after all "just a movie." Something has to happen; it must come into your eyes and affect you.

q. What are your future projects?

a. One film I want to do very much is based on a book called *The Looters.* Hopefully, I'll produce and direct it for Cinema Center. It's a kind of gangster picture, a thriller. It's the story of a bank robbery and its effect on a small town, the Mafia, and the FBI. I'm going to try to make a movie that never lets up. No build-up, start right out with a fifteen-minute bank robbery, then no let-up. It has a lot of coincidence, but I'm beginning not to mind coincidence in movies. Someone once said to Chaplin, "This is a lousy scene. Don't you think it's too much of a coincidence?" Chaplin said, "Do you think it's convenient?" The guy said, "No." Chaplin said, "Well, then it's all right. I don't mind coincidence. Life is coincidence." This would be a bigger production than *Targets.* About a million dollars. It'll be a regular picture. You know: a *movie.* For people. For a movie company. The executive producer might want to make an exposé of the Mafia. All right, but I'm more interested in making an exciting picture. By the way, they originally wanted Don Siegel to direct but couldn't get him, so he recommended me, which was a great compliment. It'll have a Siegel quality.

I'm anxious to do a few other things. *Death on the Sixth Day* would be a great suspense story involving a cross-country chase. It's from a book by the man who wrote *What Ever Happened to Baby Jane?* Another possible project is *The Last Picture Show* based on a novel by Larry Mc-Murtry. It takes place in a small Texas town during the early 1950's and you'd see the decline of a small town symbolized by the gradual degeneration of its movie house. The soundtrack would be all songs from that period—"The Hit Parade," etc. What I'm most excited about, though, is a project on Hollywood from 1909 to the present. It's about a Dwan-Griffith-like figure: great instinctive genius done to death by the system, self-consciousness. . . .

Also, Hawks has indicated he might produce some pictures that I'd direct. You know, Hawks said a wonderful thing about some of the action scenes in *Targets.* He said, "That stuff's good, and that stuff's hard to do." That to me was the ultimate compliment.

FILMOGRAPHY

Born July 30, 1939, in Kingston, New York. Bogdanovich was credited Assistant to the Director and uncredited for second-unit direction and scriptwriting on *The Wild Angels* (Roger Corman, 1966). In 1966 he worked on *Voyage to the Planet of Prehistoric Women* (originally titled *Gill-Women of Venus*), a Film Group Production released in 1969 by American International Pictures. Bogdanovich conducted the interview sequences for *The Great Professional—Howard Hawks,* a 1967 one-hour BBC-TV documentary edited by Nicholas Garnham. He is producing, writing, and directing *Directed by John Ford* (1970), a ninety-minute color documentary for the American Film Institute which will include interviews with John Wayne, James Stewart, Henry Fonda, George O'Brien, and will be climaxed by an interview with John Ford in Monument Valley. Bogdanovich is currently preparing the script for his next film, *The Looters,* based on the book by John Reese, to be shot in winter 1970 as a Cinema Center Film production. He also is preparing a major study of Orson Welles to be published in spring 1970.

Targets—1968 (90 minutes)

Producer: Peter Bogdanovich. *Script:* Peter Bogdanovich, story by Bogdanovich and Polly Platt. *Photography:* Laszlo Kovacs. *Cast:* Boris Karloff (Byron Orlok), Tim O'Kelly (Bobby Thompson), Nancy Hsueh (Jenny), James Brown (Mr. Thompson), Sandy Baron (Kip Larkin), Peter Bogdanovich (Sammy Michaels).

Arthur Penn

INTRODUCTION

Before *Bonnie and Clyde,* Arthur Penn was a relatively unknown film director with successful television ("The Colgate Comedy Hour," "Philco Playhouse," "First Person," "Playhouse 90") and theater (*Toys in the Attic, All the Way Home, An Evening with Nichols and May, Golden Boy, Wait Until Dark*) credentials. His films included three commercial flops (*The Left-Handed Gun, Mickey One, The Chase*) and a single hit, *The Miracle Worker,* which owed a large portion of its success to its popularization on the stage. Penn was left alone by Warner Brothers to make *Bonnie and Clyde,* mainly because of their predominant worries over the concurrent and costly production of *Camelot.* Initially dubious about the finished product, Warners was astonished when *Bonnie and Clyde* turned into a tremendous commerical and critical success, and Penn suddenly became one of the most prominent American directors to emerge in the last decade.

The interview centers mainly on *Bonnie and Clyde*. Despite the critical attention the film has received, we hope this interview will clear up some of the misconceptions, most notably those of critics who insist that the film is an attempted re-creation of the Dust Bowl era and/or the story of a budding Al Capone and his bloodthirsty moll. It should be noted that the themes and styles of *Bonnie and Clyde* were developed in Penn's previous films, and the interview touches upon them to illustrate that point. In short, *Bonnie and Clyde* bears more relation to *The Left-Handed Gun* or *The Chase* than to either *The Grapes of Wrath* or *Little Caesar.*

In the five films he has made thus far, Penn has been striving to create a modern anti-mythology of outcasts, in which he defines the world of his films not so much by its social heroes as by a group of titanic deviants and their disparate hangers-on. If social heroes reflect the dreams of society, Penn seems to imply, the anti-social outcasts reflect its nightmares, laced with destructive fantasies, paranoia, and sexual frustration.

In accordance with this anti-mythic conception, Penn's films and their characters are grounded not so much in a set of abstract criteria as in an intense physicality. Billy the Kid's slow-witted, intuitive, bear-like movements in *The Left-Handed Gun,* Mickey's stumbling, impulsive gestures in *Mickey One,* Calder's weary, almost static posture in *The Chase,* Clyde's limp and smirk in *Bonnie and Clyde*—these concrete details describe the characters much more eloquently than does the dialogue. The physicality both defines and limits the world of the outcasts. Penn's characters act as if they are trapped in the shells of their bodies, much like the worms in a Mexican jumping bean. The struggle to express their aspirations and exaggerations is realized not in transcendent abstractions (as might be the case with a true mythic hero) but in a compressed and distorted release of physical action, which only reminds them of their prison. Frustration is ·a key factor in Penn's work, and violence is its expression.

Similarly, violence and physical pain are the symptoms and manifestations of all moral realizations and progressions in Penn's films. In *Mickey One,* Castle's crushing of a glass ball in his hand is the expression of his guilt, and Mickey's cathartic beating allows him to face the audition and, possibly, his death. In *The Chase,* Rogers' beating of the Negro changes our response to him from pity to condemnation, and Calder's beating of the assassin releases the audience's tension only to demonstrate a complete helplessness through the inefficacy of violent action. In *Bonnie and Clyde,* the agonized death of Buck Barrow deromanticizes the mythic conception which has been set for the outlaws, just as their death at the end will partially vindicate it. Again, an abstract element is denied, and even the overblown metaphysical vagaries of *Mickey One,* Penn's most unsuccessful film to date, are somewhat redeemed by being rooted in a very immediate and physical fear of death.

Penn's visual style conveys this desire for concreteness and immediacy. For a self-admitted Welles-influenced director, Penn tends to concentrate an unusually large portion of his action in the foreground of the shot (this perhaps accounts for his enthusiasm over the telephoto lens in the interview). Jagged lines and large, coherent blocks of people and décor dominate his compositions. The somewhat blatant and very literal quality of his imagery also becomes more understandable in this context. For example, after introducing the Biblical quote, "through a glass darkly," in *The Left-Handed Gun,* Penn proceeds to show us Billy the Kid looking through a dark glass. Similarly, the car-wrecker ("The crush-out. Total Death.") in *Mickey One,* the horse running across the road in *The Chase,* and the gun-potency equations in *Left-Handed Gun* and *Bonnie and Clyde* make up in force what they lack in subtlety. This disarming directness sometimes becomes awkward and visually verbose, as in the picnic scene of *Bonnie and Clyde,* where Penn uses filters and a distorted soundtrack *and* slow-motion to express nostalgia. (In contrast, a director less concerned with immediacy, such as John Ford, can evoke the same feeling with a single receding diagonal in one of his shots.) However, Penn's justification is perhaps in the charming and eerie scene in *The Left-Handed Gun* where Billy and his sidekicks prepare to shoot a man named Moon by shooting at the moon, or in a corresponding scene in *Bonnie and Clyde,* where Clyde and the dispossessed farmer try to retaliate against the bank by shooting at the abandoned house. Imagery on a less immediate level would be false to the world of the characters.

Penn's films are as exciting and inventive on a physical level as they are slightly pretentious and unresolved on an abstract level. Since Penn is making films, the first level ultimately compensates for the second.

The following interview was conducted at Mr. Penn's office on Broadway in November 1967, three months after the release of *Bonnie and Clyde.*

M.R.

INTERVIEW

Penn: I would say that the only people who really interest me are the outcasts from society. The people who are *not* outcasts—either psychologically, emotionally, or physically—seem to me good material for selling breakfast food, but they're not material for films. What I'm really trying to say through the figure of the outcast is that a society has its mirror in its outcasts. A society would be wise to pay attention to the people who do not belong in it if it wants to find out what its configuration is and where it's failing.

q. In *The Chase* and *Bonnie and Clyde,* the fates of these char-

acters get progressively darker. It's hopeless for them to make their self-determined lives last.

a.   Well, I don't think there's anything like an even battle between the outcast and his society. But this is the *only* battle these people can fight. The odds are clearly against them. The odds have always been, as far as I can figure, against the people who seem to be on the right side. My sympathies lie with that person who cannot accommodate himself to society and may have to lose his life to change it.

q.   Toward the end of the film, Bonnie tells Clyde that she's "got the blues." At one point she had thought they were "going somewhere," and now she wonders if they are. Are they?

a.   No. I'm not holding up Bonnie and Clyde as particularly interesting outcasts nor as outcasts who have an intention or a continuous motivating line. I don't think they did. I think they were wandering, hopeless people. But I think it was a wandering, hopeless time. The time itself didn't know where it was going. The Depression was peculiarly naive. The banks did naive things. They foreclosed as many farms as they possibly could, leaving the land without anyone to farm it, which promptly broke the banks. Everyone seemed to have a sense of destination, and yet when they came to confront their lives, they discovered that this sense had departed. They found they were simply acting out whatever roles they had originally set in motion.

In the film, it was very important for me to have at least Bonnie understand that she was no longer acting out of the early promises of

Clyde—like "I'm going to dress you up, and we're going to go to the fanciest restaurants." That was gone, and they were down to a very threadbare basis. But her only place for existence was with him and in doing these things. She was perfectly willing to accept that, knowing that death was implicit in it and liable to come at any time. In that sense, it was an existential realization, and it was an important one for me.

q. These outcasts are often famous criminals, such as Billy the Kid and Bonnie and Clyde, and they seem to attract hero-worshippers. I'm thinking particularly of the Hurd Hatfield character in *Left-Handed Gun* and C. W. Moss in *Bonnie and Clyde*. Why should criminals become idols?

a. I think that outcasts who become prominent immediately have satellites who idolize them. It's a part of the bizarre character of the world that these outcasts find their historians and documentarians in these outcasts.

The character of Hurd Hatfield in *Left-Handed Gun** was constantly confronted with a myth he had formed in his own mind about Billy the Kid. His grave disappointment when he found out what Billy actually was, and his inability to reconcile those two, caused him eventually to betray Billy. The need to have heroes be genuinely heroic seems to me to be an absurdity and a foolish intention, and when somebody like the Hatfield character is let down, his revenge has no limit.

C. W. Moss does not fall into the same category because he was a fellow without imagination to whom these people brought one little bit of imagination and romance. He was perfectly willing and grateful to have that in his life.

q. Then why does he help his father set up the ambush of Bonnie and Clyde?

* *The Left-Handed Gun.* Billy (Paul Newman), a childlike outlaw, is befriended by a kindly Scottish cattleman. When the Scotsman is murdered, Billy tracks down the killers and brutally avenges the death of his friend. He is protected by Pat Garrett and a Mexican blacksmith. He alienates both of them by disrupting the former's wedding and sleeping with the latter's wife. Billy is finally betrayed by an itinerant huckster (Hurd Hatfield) who had once idolized him. Trapped, Billy forces Pat Garrett to shoot him by drawing on an empty holster.

a. I took that to mean that he was really testing his fantasy of these people to its limit—his utter belief that they would really walk on water and elude any ambush his pedestrian father could set up. He was absolutely certain that these figures out of romance would be able to walk away from it. In that sense, and only in that sense, it has a certain resemblance to the Hatfield experience in *Left-Handed Gun*—just the disparity between reality and his desire to endow Bonnie and Clyde with characteristics that they didn't necessarily have.

q. Why did you give such emphasis to the long pan using the telephoto lens ending in the shot of C.W.'s father and Sheriff Hamer sitting in the ice-cream parlor?

a. That was meat and potatoes, meat and potatoes! There was a great deal of head-shaking and breast-beating about that shot. They said, "A 400mm shot! It'll shake, and nothing's going to have any depth of field!" All the while I kept saying, "Yeah, tell me more, tell me more." And, by God, it came out looking just the right way. Of course! It's *sensational* dramatically!

At a certain point, a dramatic event can be only two-dimensional, and anything else is a lie. In this kind of schematic betrayal, we weren't interested in what they were specifically saying or what they were doing or what was going on. It was a pure act, a human act, and it should have been as two-dimensional as it's possible to get. If I had my choice, I'd go back and shoot it on an 800mm lens, right now!

The 400mm is a very exciting lens, particularly to intercut with. Everybody keeps saying that you can't intercut with it, but not only *can* you intercut, you *should*. The changes in visual experience between a telephoto lens and a lens with a great depth of field are just marvelous! I'll probably use that lens a great deal. I'm already seeing my next picture with so many scenes visualized in that way.

q. One of the most lyrical scenes in *Bonnie and Clyde* occurs when the two finally sleep together, and it comes late in the picture, so close to their destruction. Why there?

a. I'm not entirely sure that was the right thing to do—to have them consummate a relationship which was, to a sizable degree, predicated on his impotence. But it seemed to me that a credible case could be made for a man who, having been terrified of women and sexual intimacy all his life, finally finds a woman who has completely severed all her connections with the world, including the one with her family and her mother. This woman throws her lot in with him to the extent that she becomes so unthreatening that he might conceivably be able to consummate a relationship with her. That's open to quarrel, and some people have quarreled with it for being excessively romantic. It might indeed suffer under some scrutiny.

But we were also saying something else. In Hollywood pictures, the entire sexual level of existence is usually this: The actor finally makes it. It's always spectacular; it's always marvelous. There are never any mistakes. There is never any anxiety. There's never any unhappiness associated with it. It's always perfect! I mean, if you can *once* get in bed with Doris Day, it's gravy from there on in—which is a *patent lie*. That was one of the things we wanted to address ourselves to in the film.

The other thing, which is very obscure but which has some meaning to me, is that there is a certain, it seems to me, male fantasy. In the case of the male virgin, it is the dark side of the virginity, which is: if I lose my virginity, I will die. I didn't in any way mean to make that explicit, but at least it's something that was operating for me as a demonstration of an ultimate naiveté in this outcast.

q. But Clyde does die . . .

a. Yes, he does. We were not trying to alter that kind of fantasy. If anything, we were substantiating the mythic character of it: So and so did so and so; he climbed Mount Olympus . . . and he died. It's common in mythology. Prometheus brought fire to man and then was chained to the mountain and had his liver torn out. I think people endow mythical characters with those capacities: both to ascend the heights and be leveled again. I would say, though, that *every* man has his own periods when he seems to ascend the heights, but the general experience afterward is quite a lonely, desperate, pessimistic one.

q. About this love and death theme—do you think a similar and even more explicit situation exists in *Left-Handed Gun?* When Billy first makes love to the girl, he walks away, turns around, and pretends he's drawing a gun. When he dies, he makes the same gesture—the pretense of shooting a gun.

a. Yes. It was the same character, the same *sexual* character, in that picture as in *Bonnie and Clyde*. That theme is associated for me with the outcast character. It is related to the man who would view entry into the woman as entry into society—as a kind of relaxation of his abilities to remain out at the edge. The edge of his anti-social desires might be blunted by the sexual act. It's meant to be true in both cases, since both Billy and Clyde are outlaws—different, let me say, from *The Chase,* where I didn't think of Bubber as an outlaw.

q. Why does Bubber come home after his escape from prison? A sort of blind force seems to be driving him toward that town.

a. I don't really have an answer to that. We didn't have a good answer to that for a whole year. We kept raising the issue, but none of it really held water, and it doesn't hold water on the screen.

q. Do you think a similar blind force drives Mickey One or Bonnie and Clyde?

a. No. Bonnie and Clyde have a very specific force driving them. They set up a set of circumstances, and the circumstances eventuate in something beyond their expectations, which throws them outside of the law.

Mickey* was a very different character in that sense. Only one force was driving Mickey—I wish there'd been more—the feeling of having become the outcast and wanting to re-enter. The only thing he couldn't stand was to be outside of society. That was intolerable to him—to have anonymity, to be identityless. In that sense, Mickey is a less interesting and, for me, less heroic character than either Billy or Bonnie and Clyde.

   q. Do you think the relations between Bubber and Anna in *The Chase†* prefigure that between Bonnie and Clyde?

   * *Mickey One.* Mickey One (Warren Beatty), a successful nightclub comedian, is suddenly and inexplicably threatened by a nameless crime and a faceless mob. He runs away and tries to bury himself in the slums of Chicago, working in honky-tonk dives. He is asked to audition for a spot in a classier nightclub, but, thinking this is an effort by the mob to draw him out of hiding, he flees. After a cathartic beating, he returns to face the audition, presided over by a huge, blinding spotlight, and frees himself of his anxieties.

   † *The Chase.* A listless Texas town is controlled by a Big Daddy oil baron, Val Rogers (E. G. Marshall). Not only is the town aggravated by the escape of Bubber Reeves (Robert Redford) from the state prison, but the situation is complicated by the fact that Bubber's wife, Anna (Jane Fonda), has taken up with Rogers' son (James Fox). A boozed-up Saturday-night mob traps Bubber in a junkyard. Although Calder (Marlon Brando), a ded-

a. No. I don't think they can be compared. I think, in very simple terms, that Bubber came home to commit suicide. He had no ego left. He had no real destiny left. And he knew that the relationship with his wife was, to all intents and purposes, non-existent. So he came home, and it was a suicidal act.

I don't think Bonnie and Clyde were motivated out of a suicidal desire. They were motivated out of a more naive view of the world: that better things could be achieved. That she could wear a silk dress and go into the Adolphus Hotel. That he could set to rights the poor, foreclosed farmer. That he could, in a sense, level out part of the injustices of his society. The thing got out of their control; that is the sadness of it.

q. Could you elaborate on this suicidal theme? Near the end of *The Chase,* Bubber's talking about why he couldn't stand it in prison, and he says, "When you're willing to die, then you're really free." How willing is Mickey One to die at the end of that film?

a. He would accept death, but very unwillingly. The point up

icated sheriff, rescues him, Bubber is assassinated before Calder can return him to jail. Rogers' son dies as a result of the mob's violence, and Calder, giving the town up for lost, resigns his position and leaves.

until then is that he was not able to accept it. He was in flight from the possibility of his death. By the end of the picture he is not. And that's all the distance the picture traverses. It takes him from the inability to accept the possibility of his death to his ability to risk dying rather than staying outside society any longer. This society nourished him, because it was essentially a give-and-take: he was a comedian, and he needed response.

    q.   And Billy the Kid? He seems the most suicidal.

    a.   Yes, I think Billy the Kid is. Billy was afflicted with a sense of justice that he never saw acted upon in his society. He had an almost psychopathic sense of what was just and unjust. And he appointed himself judge, jury, and hangman for those who violated his sense of justice.

He had an infantile sense of justice, a kind of pre-Oedipal sense of justice: an inability to reconcile that someone had *really* slept with his mother, so that these men were constantly transgressors. They were constantly failing his system of justice, his unbearable system of justice.

At the end of the picture, he becomes the transgressor. When he sleeps with the woman, the wife of the man who has been his protector, he seals his own fate by doing the very act for which he has been punishing people all through the film.

    q.   How real is the world in which Bonnie and Clyde are living?

Do you think such a completely self-shaped existence is possible any more?

   a. I don't think it was possible even then. We delineated a world which wasn't an actual documentary vision of the world as it was then. We stripped away almost all the extraneous details we could. The visual essence of the picture is what it leaves out, for the most part. This barrenness was intentional. I don't think that for a minute we were creating any kind of real world or society. We were creating the world as two narcissistic, mutually-involved kids might view it: as a series of targets or objects which might motivate them to attack the targets. The movie is, in that sense, an abstraction rather than a genuine reportage.

   q. More specifically, how real are the characters of Bonnie and Clyde and how real is the way they chose to live: this robbing of banks and then running away. How long could this actually keep going? The

use of the poem—the legend of Bonnie and Clyde—makes there seem something more mythic than real about their existence.

   a. Oh, I think they had a strong mythic sense about themselves. Anyway, she surely did. I don't think he did. I think he was kind of a clod. Even though her ballads are doggerel, they show she had an ability to confront her situation in a more honest way than he was ever able to.

I don't know, I suppose they could have gone on robbing banks. They were petty thieves at heart. J. Edgar Hoover may take exception, but I don't think of them as killers. I don't think they set out with that intention. They really set out to level things out a little bit. The banks had the money; they didn't have the money. That just didn't seem right to them. So they decided to get a little bit of it. That was how they attracted C.W. into their orbit. Then he provided the ridiculous instrument by which they created their first murder. Having created it, they were committed to a course of action that was really larger than they were. Murder was in a certain sense bigger than these two characters. They were more thieves than murderers. They killed accidentally and they continued to kill accidentally.

q. There also seems a certain accidental, indifferent manner in the way they themselves get killed. Even the way the film ends seems to reflect this. It just stops, rather than coming to a more obvious, dramatic resolution.

a. Yes, the mood of the ending was intentional. It was an affectless death. Sheriff Hamer didn't have any strong feeling about them.

He wasn't operating inside any code or any system of honor or morality. He had his job to do. They had their job to do. And that seems to me to be the worst kind of killing there is.

It seemed to me an excessively thorough death. You know: the man who summoned all his resources to break the butterfly on the rack. Their death was the righteous indignation of a certain segment of society acted out so that it becomes at least as ugly as anything the victims of their attack might have done. The justice meted out by the forces of law and order often seems to me far worse than the crimes they're avenging, and this was one of those instances.

The death of Bonnie and Clyde in the film was literally and historically accurate. They *did* fire a thousand rounds. Eighty-seven distinct hits were found on their bodies. As recently as 1946 the car was toured around the Southwest and shown at carnivals: The Death Car of Bonnie and Clyde. It's a kind of gothic, grotesque behavior, and I would be hard-pressed at this point to make any choices between Sheriff Hamer and Bonnie and Clyde. I think I'd choose Bonnie and Clyde.

q. A very powerful, almost cathartic sense of violence runs

through your films whenever these outcast characters are confronted by the society which they're running away from or trying to change. Do you consider this violence a significant element within the films?

a. Within the films and within me. I think I would like to knock a lot of heads together, a lot of heads, and that's how I do it, in my films. I think that society could use a lot of heads knocked together.

q.   Your films give a very strong sense that this is the only way society can be changed.

a.   I'm afraid that's what I believe, sad to say. I believe in all kinds of pacific means, but if I really search deeply, I don't have a great deal of faith that they will work. I do have a certain belief that muscle will work, that some heads knocked together will work. Whenever I see the need for social change, it seems to me that the defenders of the status quo are the most resilient, impenetrable bastions. They're so difficult to assault that I find a certain persuasion in those people who counsel violence, who really *act* with a certain violence. I mean, when I see the faces of the fat, grinning sheriffs in Philadelphia or Mississippi, reason departs. All I want to do is get one of my heroes out of the movie to let 'em have it!

q.   Your style often reflects this violence. For instance, the opening of *Bonnie and Clyde* is jarring visually. What were you trying to achieve in those very oppressive close-ups at the beginning—of Bonnie undressing and later of Bonnie and Clyde after they meet?

a.   It didn't have a great deal of meaning to me. It was really just a choice of technique. In that opening, I thought: where I really want to open up and see the landscape is when the two of them get together and get in the car . . . and head out! That's where I want to see what field they're really operating on. Previous to that, the only field, it seems to me, is the look in the eye, and the shape of the lips around a Coke bottle. So I just decided to get in there as close as I possibly could. Really a fairly simple-minded choice.

q.   You seem to be preoccupied with cars. Key scenes in both *Mickey One* and *The Chase* are set in auto junkyards, and *Bonnie and Clyde* takes place almost exclusively in cars. Do you see these vehicles as symbols of modern life?

a.   No, I really don't. When we were trying to think of a place for the ending of *The Chase,* the automobile junkyard seemed natural to me. I wanted to get a kind of jungle feeling, whatever the jungle equivalent would be for this society.

The reason we relied on the automobile in *Bonnie and Clyde* has a

certain historical base. As one of the more sympathetic observers said about Bonnie and Clyde (the real Bonnie and Clyde, not the characters in the film), they were invented by the V-8 engine. In a certain sense, that was true. When Ford came out with the V-8's, the majority of the police still had the old 6's, the old Model T's and Model A's. Bonnie and Clyde would inevitably steal a V-8, a powerful car which could permit them not only to outrun the police of any local community but also to move across state borders. That was their pattern. It was not unusual for them to drive seven and eight hundred miles in one night. They were peregrinating souls on a very desperate level, and right at the head of it was that engine that was really driving them. The automobile became their province. The inside of it became their home. They would pick up people and drive them several hundred miles for conversation and society. That's why we included the scene of the undertaker and his girl. Bonnie and Clyde picked them up because they had nobody else to talk to.

    q.   There is a strong emphasis on childhood in your films. You said that Billy the Kid is a child, and Bonnie and Clyde seem childlike in their naiveté. This issue comes to a head in *The Chase*, where the initial situation arises out of Bubber's childlike need to return and the childishness of the town's reaction.

a. Probably the only really adult figure in *The Chase* was Sheriff Calder, Marlon Brando. He was a man whose whole action in the picture was to hold onto a mature view and avoid an infantile, retaliatory aggressive stance. He had to try to cool it as best he could in a community which was somewhat infantile in its views. The sadness of that story is that Calder failed. The other sadness is that we failed Calder. We failed Brando because we didn't dramatize that nearly well enough, and that to me was the conspicuous failure of the film. Calder was an interesting character with a fascinating motive, but we stepped all over our feet trying to get that on the screen.

q. In the sense that Calder fails, it seems that none of these outcasts, these figures in direct conflict with society, are capable of really changing it. I think this feeling is expressed in the scene where Bonnie and Clyde and the dispossessed farmer and his worker are taking potshots at the abandoned house, taken over by the banks. They're firing at it, trying to get back at it, but they really can't.

a. Yes. I don't think outcasts or people who engage in these acts of violence can necessarily effect change. I think, however, that they have no other choice. And I think that only with a vision of history can we see that *maybe,* in some nutty way, they really did effect change. But *at the time,* I don't think we can ever point to change. I mean, more change has probably been accomplished by Gandhi than by Jesse James or

William Tell. But maybe that's only true in certain circumstances. In other circumstances, I think some people have had to fight the fight and lose the fight, to create a kind of conscience that is part of the rest of us for the rest of our lives. In that respect, it's fortunate that these people do their thing.

q.   The actors in your films are always given very strong physical characterizations. We remember certain details in their appearance or mannerisms which are visually powerfully delineated. How closely do you work with your actors in getting this kind of effect?

a.   Pretty closely. I really have a lot to do with that. I like kinetic behavior; I think that's good for cinema. Kinetic—Cinema: the two words have the same source. I think it's good cinema to have somebody *walk* in a certain way and *move* in a certain way. After all, you're showing a distillation; you're showing some ninety minutes out of a lifetime. So somebody had better come through a door or hit a desk or fire a gun in a *very* particular way for it to be meaningful.

For example, I thought Warren's limp was a very important factor in forming Clyde's character . . . the dialect, the whole gait. Also, Warren always wore that gun under his jacket, whether it was needed in the scene or not. He never played a scene without it, never, because he felt it was so much a part of his character. And it *did* make his suit fit in a certain way; it made him stand in a certain way. I think these things have peripheral benefits that we may not be conscious of, but they do help convey character.

q.   Does this visual factor affect you when you're casting?

a.   Oh yes. Why not have attractive people? I must say I've come a long way in that department. When I first started out, I felt that films had to be about really ordinary-looking people. But, by God, they're not ordinary! They're sixty feet high! That's one incontrovertible fact about the movie screen, and somebody not very attractive and sixty feet high is *really* ugly.

q.   How much freedom do you give your actors?

a.   Well, it's always relative. What I try to do is create the climate of accident, of controlled accident. Certain things I set very meticulously. Other things I will not set, but alter from take to take so as to throw the actors off. For instance, although they're sitting in chairs, on the next take maybe one chair leg will be a little shorter than the others. Something will happen to cause them to say, "Jesus Christ, I'm doing a shot, but at the same time this chair doesn't . . ." They have to deal with that. It's by taking them unaware, with some of the physical conditions of living, that I try to create these accidents.

q. In general, do you think you have as much freedom working with studios as you would want? Were you able to do as much with *Bonnie and Clyde,* as a Warner Brothers production, as you wanted?

a. Yes. After the fact, I would have to say that we were not limited by the studio at all. However, during the making of it, there was always the possibility that a very severe imposition of limits could have taken place . . .

q. I take it this was true of *The Chase.*

a. Yes. It not only could have taken place, but it *did* take place—totally.

Fortunately, studios are growing up now. They are recognizing that the nature of film is changing, and that they have to give the people who make the films the opportunity to put them together in their own way. In my next film, for instance, I had no difficulty in getting the right to cut it in New York, the right to cut it in my own way. There has been no interference at all. Studios are disappearing as studios and becoming what they have always been in true character: financing organizations. They're business organizations, and any pretentions toward the aesthetic are only the reflections of some elderly, vain men.

q. Do you still enjoy working with theater?

a. Yes, I enjoy the theater a lot. I don't know that I enjoy working with Broadway theater; I think it's silly. Something can be learned about distillation in theater that's very important. Also, good actors come from the theater. I found Estelle Parsons and Gene Hackman at a summer stock theater in Stockbridge.

q. Do you think there's as much room for personal expression in theater direction as in film?

a. No. But I don't think a great deal is wrong with not having personal expression sometimes. Something can be said for technical craft, for the ability to elucidate someone else's work.

More and more I'm learning to get rid of the disciplines of the theater when I'm making a film. In the theater, the script is embalmed. It is The Text, a revered work. A man's written it, and it's meant to be delivered as such. In the cinema, the dialogue is only a guide. My writer friends are often offended by the literary level of the scripts of my films. On the other hand, I keep thinking it doesn't matter a great deal, and I'm sort of offended sometimes by the *look* of their plays.

An awful lot of vanity is inherent in the movie-making event. It's a seductive event. Seldom in one's fantasies can one achieve the kind of power that you have on a movie set. Power corrupts; movie power corrupts absolutely. Dialogue in the cinema only serves as a guide to a kind of visualization, and if this be megalomania, so be it. There is only one event in making movies, and that's the director's event. It's not any-body else's. I don't care how well written the script is. You can get into a motel room in Texas, and the dialogue can be exquisite, but what you choose to look at and how you look at it is everything. I mean, I can show you tons of out-takes where I looked at the wrong thing, and I can only say that had the movie been made up of those out-takes, it would have been dreadful. You know, it's perfectly possible to not see something in the right way. That's the whole thing; it's really a cyclops experience. You get that one glassy eye with which you see everything, and that's movies.

FILMOGRAPHY

Born September 27, 1922 in Philadelphia, Pennsylvania. In addition to the films listed below, Penn worked on *The Train* (1963); after one week of shooting exteriors, he was replaced by John Frankenheimer.

The Left-Handed Gun—1957 (102 minutes)
Producer: Fred Coe. *Script:* Leslie Stevens, from the play by Gore Vidal. *Photography:* J. Peverell Marley. *Cast:* Paul Newman (William "Billy the Kid" Bonney), John Dehner (Pat Garrett), Hurd Hatfield (Moultrie), Lita Milan (Celsa), James Best (Tom Folliard), James Congdon (Charlie Boudre), Colin Keith-Johnston (Tunstall), Denver Pyle (Ollinger).

The Miracle Worker—1962 (106 minutes)
Producer: Fred Coe. *Script:* William Gibson, from his play. *Photography:* Ernest Caparros. *Cast:* Anne Bancroft (Annie Sullivan), Patty Duke (Helen Keller), Victor Jory (Captain Keller), Inga Swenson (Kate Keller), Andrew Prine (James Keller).

Mickey One—1964 (93 minutes)
Producer: Arthur Penn, Harrison Starr. *Script:* Alan Surgal. *Photography:* Ghislain Cloquet. *Cast:* Warren Beatty (Mickey), Alexandra Stewart (Jenny), Hurd Hatfield (Castle), Franchot Tone (Ruby Lapp),

Teddy Hart (Berson), Jeff Corey (Fryer), Kamatari Fujiwara (The Artist).

The Chase—1965 (138 minutes)

Producer: Sam Spiegel. *Script:* Lillian Hellman, from the novel and play by Horton Foote. *Photography:* Joseph LaShelle. *Cast:* Marlon Brando (Sheriff Calder), Jane Fonda (Anna Reeves), Robert Redford (Bubber Reeves), E. G. Marshall (Val Rogers), Angie Dickinson (Ruby Calder), Janice Rule (Emily Stewart), James Fox (Jake Rogers), Miriam Hopkins (Mrs. Reeves), Martha Hyer (Mary Fuller), Richard Bradford (Damon Fuller), Robert Duvall (Edwin Stewart), Henry Hull (Mr. Briggs).

Bonnie and Clyde—1967 (111 minutes)

Producer: Warren Beatty. *Script:* David Newman and Robert Benton. *Photography:* Burnett Guffey. *Cast:* Warren Beatty (Clyde Barrow), Faye Dunaway (Bonnie Parker), Michael J. Pollard (C. W. Moss), Gene Hackman (Buck Barrow), Estelle Parsons (Blanche), Denver Pyle (Frank Hamer), Dub Taylor (Ivan Moss), Gene Wilder (Eugene Grizzard).

Alice's Restaurant—1969 (110 minutes)

Producer: Hillard Elkins, Joe Manduke. *Script:* Venable Herndon and Arthur Penn. *Photography:* Michael Nebbia. *Cast:* Pat Quinn (Alice), Arlo Guthrie (Arlo), James Broderick (Ray), Michael Mc-Clanathan (Shelley), Kathleen Dabney (Karen), Pete Seeger.

Samuel Fuller

INTRODUCTION

Samuel Fuller is perhaps the most aggressive of all film-makers. His films are concerned with the direct physical and visual communication of emotional impact. In a review of *The Naked Kiss,* critic Michael Delahaye in *Cahiers du Cinema* made an observation which could apply to all of Fuller's films: "Let he who is not a ghost dare to say he has felt nothing."

Fuller puts in his films pimps, swindlers, gangsters, prostitutes, petty crooks, stool pigeons, detectives—people on the lower border of society. The fringe position of these characters makes them easily detachable from the mainstream of social concerns, and thus allows them to act out Fuller's favorite drama: the conflict between personal, emotional interests and the more impersonal, mechanical responses social and environmental superstructures demand.

This police-blotter lineup of characters gives Fuller's stories the flavor of back-page features in newspapers like the *Daily News* or the *Evening Graphic,* for which Fuller was once a reporter. For example, here is *The Naked Kiss* in tabloid headlines: "EX-CALL GIRL KILLS

MILLIONAIRE FIANCE!" We recognize the potential depersonalization of these stories into the protective clichés which newspaper headlines symbolize (e.g., "150 PEOPLE KILLED IN PLANE CRASH"). However, Fuller's forceful, violent presentation of the material erases the comfortable distance we like to establish between ourselves and the medium. In his recent films, *The Crimson Kimono, Underworld, U.S.A., Shock Corridor,* and *The Naked Kiss,* Fuller shows a complete command of the means necessary to shake the most complacent audience out of its habitual apathy.

The director's commitment to an emotional and personal value system has led many critics to oversimplify his talent as "primitive." This conception would be more viable if Fuller eschewed all concerns other than those personal ones he prefers. However, Fuller's world-view encompasses with equal depth all aspects of the conflict he presents. The outer, social frameworks which threaten his characters' emotional integrity are indicated with admirable force in nearly all of his films. In *Pickup on South Street,* the city established in ominous reflections on street windows, and the huge bridge looming outside Richard Widmark's shack, eventually become the gigantic superstructure of National Projects in *Underworld, U.S.A.,* which infects and perverts practically every level of American society—from sports and charity to familial devotion and big business.

Fuller's films depict a society in the rigor mortis of institutionalization. He calls for a complete revitalization of that society on a primal emotional level, even in the most violent manner. Fuller's visual equivalent of the personal impulse is the close-up, which he uses more frequently and more forcefully than any other film-maker. The visual rhythm throughout Fuller's films is from long-shot to close-up and then back to long-shot. Similarly, the structure of his stories goes from a long view which establishes the outer framework to closer, personal dramas, often in direct conflict with the former element, then finally back to the outer view, now re-evaluated and re-fashioned in completely personal terms. The final long-shots of the corridor in *Shock Corridor* and the route to the bus station in *The Naked Kiss* are repeated from earlier contexts in the film, but their meaning is completely changed in light of the volcanic emotional struggles which have intervened.

With the exception of *Baron of Arizona, Hell and High Water, Merrill's Marauders,* and *Shark,* Fuller has exercised virtually complete control over every aspect of his films. His personality has revealed itself consistently and progressively in all eighteen of his motion pictures. The following interview, conducted at Mr. Fuller's home in Los Angeles in November 1968, covers his career chronologically, film by film. Fuller himself believes that his best work is yet to come, and for that reason we have included, at the end of the interview, his comments on various projects he has conceived in recent years.

M.R.

INTERVIEW

I Shot Jesse James

q. In *I Shot Jesse James,** the John Ireland character (Robert Ford) at first strikes one as a rat, but, as the film progresses, he seems to become more sympathetic.

a. I'll make it very brief about Mr. Robert Ford. I happen to like Robert Ford, because he did something which should have been done quite a bit earlier in the life of Jesse Woodson James.

Jesse James was a half-assed homo who impersonated a girl for Quantrill's Raiders when he was fifteen. Acting as a hooker, he enticed soldiers into a little shack called "The House of Love," where these bastard raiders would kill the soldiers and rob them. When he was eighteen, Jesse and his brother held up a hospital train, wherein they killed all the casualties and robbed them.

Since I despise Mr. James (and would give my right eyeball to make the true story of Jesse James), I've always had sympathy for Robert Ford. One day, the real story of Jesse James will be made. It will shock people. Rough! Vicious! We have young squirts today who are supposed

* *I Shot Jesse James.* Bob Ford (John Ireland) murders Jesse James (Reed Hadley), his best friend. He wants the reward money because he hopes to marry Cynthy (Barbara Britten). However, he only gets a fraction of the booty, and is denounced for his treachery by the townspeople. When Cynthy is wooed by John Kelley (Preston Foster), Ford takes the job of re-enacting the murder scene in a local saloon so he can earn enough money to win back Cynthy. Disgusted with the job, Ford flees and becomes a gold prospector. When Jesse's brother Frank (Tom Tyler) tracks him down, a showdown is inevitable. However, it is Kelley who draws against Ford and kills him.

to be under the spell of narcotics, and they hold up banks and mug women. They're cream-puffs compared with these old guys. They knocked off people immediately.

q. In the picture, how well do you think Robert Ford understands his own motives when he kills Jesse?

a. Oh, he knew he'd get amnesty. He had to make a selection between freedom, a couple of dollars, a woman, and a little farm—and his friend. Being human, Ford naturally decided that the sacrificial lamb was the friend. Oh, he understood it all right. What he didn't understand, until the end of the picture, was that he walked in a daze. I tried to get a groping, not half-witted, but not too mentally alert type of a man. The last line in the picture is my story. Ireland tells the girl, "I'll tell you

something I haven't told anyone. I'm sorry I killed Jesse. I loved him." I wanted that type of an association. Robert Lippert, the man who financed the picture, didn't catch that. He just thought it was a kind of Damon-Pythias relationship, and he let it remain.

q. How much were you relying on popular knowledge of the shooting of Jesse James? From the first time you see Jesse's living room in the movie, the picture on the wall is tilted. I think that most spectators would know the popular version of Jesse's death and would respond to that.

a. Even as kids, we've all seen illustrations of Jesse being shot while adjusting a picture on the wall. I wanted to get a simplification of what we know, but I wanted it to be fresh. I tried to get the feeling of a gun and a weird room by tilting the camera. I wanted the camera to tilt slightly in one direction and the picture to tilt in another. So that when it evens out, we have death. I wanted something weird in the beginning, but when it's over, dead men are usually horizontal, and everything is

simple, on one line.

I love the West. I read a lot about the West, and I'm shocked, I'm ashamed that in pictures they have not made the true story of the winning of the West—comprising ninety per cent foreigners, one-hundred per cent laborers, nothing to do with guns. Streets, mountains, roads, bridges, streams, forests—that's the winning of the West to me. Hard! Tremendous, tremendous fight. But we have, as you know, Cowboys and Indians and all that. Shane comes into town, cleans it up, and leaves. He's doing that every week now on TV.

That's why I didn't want any horsemanship in the picture. After we finished shooting, Lippert put in some stock shots of people riding around. I didn't want that. I'm not interested in a horse story. I'm not even interested in Jesse. I'm interested in Ford, and how difficult it must be for an assassin to kill someone, especially someone he knows. How difficult!

At one time, I wanted to do the story of Brutus. I'm not interested in Caesar. I'm interested in the assassin—what makes an assassin? The night before he killed Caesar, what did Brutus think about? How did he sleep? Did he go to the can? What did he eat? Did he drink? Whom did he talk to? Did he argue? Did he get laid? What happened that night? *That,* to me, is great drama. I could do a whole movie on just that one man and what he went through that night. I tried to get that flavor with Ford in *I Shot Jesse James.*

In his next film, *The Baron of Arizona,* Fuller explored the relations between Vincent Price and Ellen Drew which somewhat anticipated the Dolores Dorn–Cliff Robertson match in *Underworld, U.S.A.* These relationships are characterized by a latent emotional commitment which is not recognized or accepted by their major characters until it is (almost) too late. (See Filmography.)

The Steel Helmet

a. I made *The Steel Helmet** in ten days. Ten days! One set. One-half a day with all the action at Griffith Park. Twenty-five university students as extras. Twenty-five men! We couldn't afford anything else.

* The Steel Helmet. Sergeant Zack's (Gene Evans) entire platoon is massacred by the North Koreans. He survives because of a freak accident involving his helmet, and is aided by a Korean orphan whom he calls Short Round. They join a platoon commanded by a rule-book lieutenant (Steve Brodie) whom Zack despises. The platoon sets up an observation post in a Buddhist temple, and they apprehend a Communist who is inside. When Short Round is killed by a sniper, Zack, in a rage, kills the Communist prisoner. In a massive attack on the temple, the lieutenant is killed while demonstrating exceptional bravery. Zack bestows his charmed helmet on the lieutenant's grave and leaves with the other three survivors.

I made them look like 350 or 400. Sometimes, when you can't afford it, you improvise, and it comes off better.

q. The relation between Sergeant Zack and the little boy is similar to the one between Price and Drew in *The Baron of Arizona*. Zack doesn't realize the boy's attachment to him until after the boy is killed . . .

a. Ah yes! I see what you mean. Any damn emotional cementing between them grows on them. Yes, you're right.

What Zack epitomized there was the symbol of a non-com: no emotion whatsoever. None! Because if you have emotions, you're not in war. There's no time for emotion. It becomes a job. You wake up. You work a little. Maybe you go on a patrol or a little skirmish line. Your fight is very brief. You rest. You crap. You eat. Then you go out and shoot again. You go to sleep. Then you get up . . .

If you do this for three years, it's just a job. It's a tremendous machine inside you. The only emotion you have is: "When do I get out of here, and when does somebody replace me?" That's the only emotion you ever experience in war. You become aware of sounds. You become aware of sight. And you become aware of trust in man. Very aware. If I know you two fellows are on my right, that's fine. If I'm worried about you, I'm in trouble.

So I thought it might be a very effective scene if Zack blows his top, not because of the enemy or shooting or all that, but because of a kid. You should never blow your top over a person who's on your side. The kid was on his side. You did catch something there; it was a growing love affair. It was a love story.

When Zack blew his top, he shot down an unarmed P.O.W. To me, that was not a shocker. But it was to the press. Tremendous shocker. A lot of editorials. I have all the newspapers. Big full-page interviews asking, "WOULD YOU SHOOT THIS MAN?" You see, I think it's a little stupid, when you're in war, to hold your fire just because a man puts his hands up. Five minutes before that, he's shooting at you. He runs out of ammunition; he can put his hands up. I mean, certainly there's no law. If there's a law in war, then we're really completely nuts. Now, we're

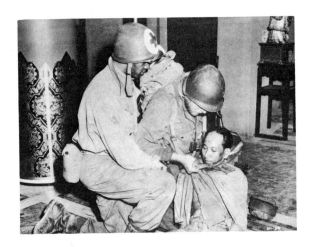

only ninety-nine per cent nuts. But if there's a law . . . How can there be a law in an illegal act?

So, I cannot get concerned about shooting a prisoner. It means nothing to me. Absolutely nothing. I think the idea of shooting a *man* is more important. I don't care whether he's a friend or an enemy. But the idea that we have laws and Geneva Conventions and rules and regulations is a cover-up for a lot of stupid things.

q. Why did you give such emphasis to the Buddha monument in the film?

a. I specifically wanted to put the blood plasma in the palm of the Buddha. I wanted to show the blood running out of his hand into the Commie. I thought it would be very touching to have death there in the lap of *his* God, and within minutes that whole temple is going to be obliterated. But still that Buddha remains.

The big Buddha in Kamakura, Japan, was surrounded by a tremendous temple. Many hundreds of years ago, there was a quake. Everything was demolished except this big Buddha. . . . Oh! You saw it in *House of Bamboo.* That's the Kamakura Buddha. I did know the story of that Buddha, and I thought it was strange that it remained. Just like the Greek relics today. I don't know why in the hell certain columns remain and certain ones don't. That's the flavor I tried to get with the Buddha in *Helmet*.

q. At the end of the film, after the major attack on the temple, the three survivors are all outcasts in some way—the Negro, the Oriental, and the bald-headed fellow. This adds a very downbeat note to the "victory" over the North Koreans.

a. I deliberately put a line in that scene which is strictly dogface dialogue. No matter what happens, when the battle is over, there's always one man who's going to say, "I'm hungry." And there's always one fellow who's ready to vomit.

But the theme of *The Steel Helmet* is the ending. That's what I wanted to show: that this was *not* the end. The wars go on and on and on. There's no end to the story. It's impossible.

Fixed Bayonets

a. In *Fixed Bayonets** I wanted to do the story of a fellow who cannot knock off an enemy soldier. In the end, when he does—out of pure fear, panic, frustration, and lack of coordination—they compliment him, and he accepts the compliment. That's what happens in war.

To me, the thrill of war—and there is a tremendous thrill—is death. That's the only thing I'm really interested in, because it's the only mystery. That's why I'll always dramatize it. I don't think anything is more dramatic in motion pictures than death, even though we assume we're cold-blooded and can take it for granted. I don't know of any other subject. At all.

I seldom heard a dying man make a speech. The general things you

***Fixed Bayonets.** When a large American force has to pull out in Korea, a rear-guard platoon is left behind to give the illusion of remaining strength. The platoon's corporal, Denno (Richard Basehart), has been psychologically unable to kill a man, and he dreads the eventuality that he may end up in command. As the Communists feel out the strength of the rear guard, the platoon's officers are picked off one by one, and Denno assumes command. By this time, the enemy has discovered the ruse, and they launch a large offensive. The platoon is able to divert the enemy long enough to allow themselves to escape, and, in the process, Denno acquires the ability to kill.

hear, when a man is hit next to you, are: "Oh no. Oh hell. Oh hell no. Ooooh noooo. Please. Please. Not me."

q. That's exactly what the "mute" soldier in *Steel Helmet* says when he's killed.

a. Oh right! That's what he says. That's what you say, and you go. That's exactly what happens. None of this: "Now, I want to tell you one thing, Joshua . . . two miles down there, you go to your left, you find Nora . . . she's got a horse waiting . . . tell her the sheriff said, 'Ichabod Crane was right.' "

It's selfish. All exits are selfish—and personal. And that's the way it should be.

q. The battle scenes in *Fixed Bayonets* are quite impressive and quite unusual: quick cuts, no sense of space or broad spectacle, very realistic and terrifying . . .

a. Very intimate, right. First of all, I had a tremendous ice machine. The set was built, and I rehearsed the actors and the stuntmen. Then I was ready to go. I told everybody, "Just leave the stage. Get a little air. Relax." Then I said, "Ice it!" That big hose just went whoosshh, and the whole set was ice. Then I called the actors back in. Were they surprised! Those falls, there's no acting in them. Didn't you get a feeling of panic? It was real. They were slipping all over the place. They knew there were explosions going on, and they had to get out of there.

See, I assign each actor a number. I'm holding a board with the corresponding numbers on it. I yell a number, and I push a button. Wham! There's an explosion. Now, when I yell "One!," I may press the number nine button. I can do that, because I know where everyone is. That gets the actors very nervous. They say, "Wait a minute! Wait a minute! Which one is my number?" I never had a serious accident, though, because I'm very careful. It's too much of a responsibility. I do admit, a couple of times, if the actor was a little slow, I had an urge to push that button. But then I said, "No, it's not worth it."

That reminds me of a funny incident on *Fixed Bayonets*. One of our stuntmen was hurt. Nothing serious, he twisted his leg. I found out that when stuntmen are hurt and taken off a picture, their salary is stopped.

So I got an idea. I told my assistant, "Use him as a casualty." Well, by the end of the week, I had a casualty list this long. Anyone who was hurt continued in the picture as a casualty. Only, they were real casualties! If a fellow couldn't walk in the picture, he really couldn't walk.

q. I liked the scene at the beginning of the picture where all the troops are pulling out, and the rear-guard platoon is left behind. They're standing there, frozen, while a very distorted, muffled melody is heard on the soundtrack.

a. I wanted a combination of "On the Banks of the Wabash" and "Taps." I thought that was a touching melody for the scene. I was very anxious to get the effect of a rear guard: the abandonment.

q. In that scene, when the troops pull out, you track across the faces of the men in the rear guard. When they cross the river at the end,

their faces all pass by the camera, and they look almost the same as at the beginning. Their situation is the same.

a. Did you get the sense of balance there? All except the ones who didn't make it.

Fuller's next film was *Park Row*. It is largely a reconstruction of

journalism's formative "romantic" era and is characterized by the frequent use of a mobile camera which tracks back and forth on Park Row between newspaper offices and past statues of Horace Greeley and Ben Franklin. (See Filmography.)

Pickup on South Street

q. The opening of *Pickup on South Street**—when Widmark picks

* *Pickup on South Street*. On a crowded subway, Skip McCoy (Richard Widmark) picks the purse of Candy (Jean Peters). Among his booty, although he does not know it at the time, is a piece of top-secret microfilm that was being passed by Candy's consort, a Communist agent (Richard Kiley). Candy discovers the whereabouts of the film through Moe Williams (Thelma Ritter), a police informer. She attempts to seduce McCoy to recover the film. She fails to get back the film and falls in love with him. The desperate agent exterminates Moe and savagely beats Candy. McCoy, now goaded into action,

135

the girl's pocketbook containing the secret information—is played without dialogue. This gives the action a great deal of ambiguity. It's only much later that you find out what actually transpired. So, instead of starting out with the "Commies vs. the Good Guys," you're primarily concerned with personal issues from the start.

a. You're right about the ambiguity. The ending is like that, too. Some people thought, "Well, I guess he'll go off with the girl and be happy." I gave her a line at the end to show that they'll never change. The cop says, "No matter what happens, I'll find this son of a bitch in a week or two with his hand in somebody's pocket." She says, "You

wanna bet?" The way she said that showed that I wanted the audience to feel he eventually will go back to picking pockets, and she'll go back to doing whatever the hell she was doing.

This is what I got a kick out of in the picture: the idea of having a pickpocket, a police informer, and a half-assed hooker as the three main characters. The picture was made in about eighteen or twenty days at Fox. A big picture for me. The whole thing was shot in downtown

---

apprehends the agent in a particularly brutal fight in a subway. McCoy and Candy, temporarily reformed, are reunited.

L.A., and I used a lot of tricks to make it look like New York.

    q. Was the subway a set?

    a. It was a set. I told the art director I wanted those stairs, because I liked the idea of Widmark pulling Kiley down by the ankles, and the heavy's chin hits every step. Dat-dat-dat-dat-dat: it's musical.

    q. Although you establish the city very forcefully in the film, you seem to be more interested in individuals than in the structures, political or otherwise, which surround the characters.

    a. Oh, sure. More than that, too. I specifically hit hard on describing Kiley not as a Communist, but as an agent. There's a big difference. Tremendous difference. An agent is a paid employee. If tomorrow another country will give him more money, he will do it for them. It's got nothing to do with party affiliation. Nothing political about it at all. But when I talked to people, even on the set, all they thought was, "Well, he's a Commie." I didn't want just that. That's too obvious.

A Commie doesn't mean to me what he does to a lot of other people. I mean, there are Communists all over the world. I even know Communists who hate other Communists. Frankly, I don't understand what they're talking about. It's all meaningless. Politics bore me, but the *politicians* do not bore me, because they're characters.

That's why I played down the political situation in *Pickup*. I was not interested in the structure. I could have had a hell of a big scene, with fifty or sixty extras. They're all gathered together, and the head man says, "This is terrible. What about the Party?" You never hear the word "Party" in my film.

You are never even told that the FBI man in *Pickup* is from the FBI. He's just from the government. I didn't want to pinpoint it. Just before I made the picture, Fuchs, the British espionage agent, had been arrested for selling information to Russia. The government man in the film says to Widmark, "You know about Fuchs. You know what he did." Widmark says, "I don't know what you're talking about. I don't care." That's the mood I wanted to get in the picture.

q. This seemed to be the most "close-up" of your films. You

even kept dollying in from a close-up to a more extreme close-up.

a. Oh yes. You noticed that? I like to do that sometimes. *Jesse James* was also shot with a lot of close-ups because I'm not interested in the bank or the people in the bank. I'm interested in a teller who is going to be shot and the man who is going to shoot him. The same thing in *Pickup*. Come to think of it, very few extras are in the film, very few people around.

q. Another technique I especially liked was the way you moved the camera. For example, at one point Widmark has to get out of his shack, and he swings across the water on a rope. Rather than simply following the action, the camera moved back before he swung. You used the same type of camera work in the long-take where Jean Peters is getting beat up by Kiley. The camera would go to where the action was going, before the action actually went there.

a. In that scene with Peters, I told the cameraman, "Give me a leeway. Make it loose enough, but fluid at all times. Don't hang around too long." I wanted that fluidity, because the camera can help the eye with action. If your camera is moving, and your action is moving—boy, you have action! If your action is moving, and your camera is stationary, it is not that effective. It's also better not to just follow the action. Again, it's your eye. I want to go beyond the eye. So you have two sets of eyes: the camera is moving, and your own eye is moving.

q. Just before the scene of Thelma Ritter's death, there's a shot of her selling her neckties in a construction area at night. I got a hellish, underworld feeling from that shot. Were you trying for this?

a. Oh no. What I wanted there was construction. I wanted something that is being born right before somebody is dead. I wanted something *alive*. I wanted one of those riveting machines and fire and lights and life. Alive! Noisy! Because it's going to be very quiet soon—for her.

q. Just as a footnote, I'd like to ask about one of my favorite bit characters: Lightnin' Louie.

a. Lightnin' Louie was played by a card expert and magician from Chicago named Victor Perry. It was his first and last picture. I just happened to meet him. I asked him, "Are you good with your hands?" He said, "Am I good? Just watch my act!" I said, "What I want in my

film is a man who is so indifferent to people that he has contempt even for the people he's selling information to—especially if they interfere with him while he's eating. That's why I want a man like you, with a big belly. Now let me see you pick up some money with the chopsticks and just keep eating with them." Did you like that touch? That's exactly why I used him.

Fuller's next film, *Hell and High Water,* was undertaken largely as an experiment in Cinemascope and is technically interesting primarily for a battle sequence involving two submarines. (See Filmography.)

House of Bamboo

a. *House of Bamboo** was the first American picture made in Japan, and the first time I really went on location. It's the only way to make a movie. I think motion pictures should really move out, have some fun.

q. The pre-credits sequence—the train holdup and the murder in the shadow of Mt. Fujiyama—was very striking.

a. I didn't want to show Mt. Fuji as you always see it—with the cherry blossoms. I wanted white against white against white. In the fore-

* *House of Bamboo.* Eddie Spanier (Robert Stack), a California police-man, is sent to Tokyo to infiltrate a crime operation run by Americans. The organization's boss, Dawson (Robert Ryan), becomes excessively protective of Spanier, even to the point of breaking the gang's policy of finishing off members who are wounded in action. Dawson's affection blinds him to Spa-nier's treachery. His organization collapses, and Dawson is killed after a psy-chopathic shooting spree in an amusement park.

ground, I wanted that *black* train. I wanted a flavor of grim bleakness. Then, as we pull away from death, the murder of the soldier, you see a woman running. The titles come on, and we start getting lush with color, little by little. By the time she's reporting to the police, we are in color! That excited me.

q. Like *Steel Helmet, House of Bamboo* is essentially a love story between two men, Stack and Ryan.

a. Definitely. That's epitomized by one line of dialogue that I gave Ryan. It comes right after the first robbery. Ryan is trying to figure out why, in Stack's case, he broke his gang's policy of killing wounded men so that they won't talk to the police. First, he says to Stack, "I don't know why I saved your neck." Then he turns to the other men and says, "Will anyone please tell me why I did it?"

That's the big line, the cementing between them. I hoped it would get people a little nervous, because it's usually a line that a man says about a woman: "Why did I marry her? What am I doing with her? Why did I go out with her? Will anyone please tell me why I did it?" That's as close as I could get to it, when Ryan says that line.

q. The way in which we judge these two characters is typical of your films. On a structural, institutional level, Stack is a police agent out to stop a crime wave, and we should sympathize with him. But on a more personal level—the male love story—Ryan is more sympathetic.

a. Oh sure. First of all, you establish sympathy by humor. If you have a straight-laced, stonefaced performance, there's no sympathy. We introduce Ryan when Stack is hit through a paper wall, and these gangsters are sitting there. Ryan starts to laugh. That's the beginning of my sympathy for the heavy.

I also told Ryan to never say "my father" but to say "pappy." Right away you have to like any guy who says "pappy," because he likes his father. When Stack talked about his family, he was dull. After all, he's not an agent; he's just a cop. Just a cop from California. Didn't mean a thing.

q. The way Ryan ran his crime syndicate was fascinating. A robbery was conducted like a military maneuver, with battle maps,

briefing sessions, reconnaissance, photographs.

a. After the war, I tried to sell Metro a story about a group of men who were in the same platoon, and when the war is over, they form a combination of criminals. They take Fort Knox, using the same military maneuver with which they knocked out a pillbox on Omaha Beach. The studio didn't buy it. So when I was asked to do *Bamboo*, I figured I'd use that situation.

Run of the Arrow

a. I wanted Steiger to play the lead in *Run of the Arrow** because he didn't look like a typical American hero. He was blubbery. I thought he would look ungainly on a horse, and he did. He was perfect for that role; he was a misfit. The Steiger character became a religious zealot as

---

* *Run of the Arrow.* Confederate soldier O'Meara (Rod Steiger) fires the last bullet of the Civil War and wounds Driscoll (Ralph Meeker). O'Meara preserves the cartridge as a keepsake. Unwilling to accept the South's defeat, he joins an Indian tribe after enduring their test of strength: the Run of the Arrow. He is eventually confronted again by the Union Army and Lieutenant Driscoll. He uses the same bullet on Driscoll a second time— to save him from torture by the Indians.

far as hatred was concerned. He acted the same way the losers act in any war, in this case the Confederates.

q. You often use a prop as more than just a symbol or a motif, but almost as a character, such as the helmet in *Steel Helmet* and the bullet in this film.

a. Yes. My original title for the film was *The Last Bullet.* That's what started me thinking about the whole story: what happened to the last cartridge fired in the Civil War? I thought it was a good title, but it sounded too much like a Western.

q. The scene in which Steiger says goodbye to his mother was brilliant in pointing up his bitterness and loneliness.

a. The Confederate in that scene who sang the song against the Constitution was played by a Southerner, whose hobby was collecting folklore and ballads. He loved it, being a Southerner and against the damn Yankees. My art director on the picture was a very virulent Yankee. I'm only telling you this because there's an evil streak in me that I like. I thought it would be wonderful to get them together in my office. I'll never forget it; it was the most wonderful moment of my life to introduce these two men who despised each other. They immediately got into a tremendous argument. I heard the whole Civil War fought all over again in my office.

q. In this film and in *Forty Guns,* you used a lot of very slow dissolves. Why?

a. That was for the mood. I wanted something beautiful, because the idea of technical, mechanical beauty (I usually don't like anything mechanical) was the only contrast I could get to the action, the violence. I tried to time each one of those dissolves so that it was almost like music, a beautiful piece of music, and I had all hell break loose right after or right before that. I couldn't have gotten any other contrast, unless I used a long talking scene, and I didn't want that.

Contrast makes emotion—that's what makes music, that's what makes painting. Rembrandt, with his color, will use beautiful, subdued black-black-blue or blue-blue-black—Jesus, you can't tell what color it is—and then there's that hot gold or red with that one light. That's

beautiful contrast. I just love that kind of stuff. I tried to get it in those long dissolves.

q. Why did you concentrate on feet rather than faces in the Run of the Arrow scene?

a. I shot that scene without my star. Steiger sprained his ankle right before we shot it, and he was taken off to the hospital. I used a

young Indian in his place. Nobody noticed it. They thought I was being highly creative, highly artistic: "Imagine! Almost a boy wonder, a genius! Sensational! The way he shot it by just showing the feet!" Well, I would have shot about eighty per cent of the scene with just feet anyway, because that's the whole idea of the Run. But occasionally I would have liked to whip up with the camera and show Steiger's face, just as I did with [Jay C.] Flippen. I could never do it, because he was in the hospital.

Joe Biroc, the cameraman, did a terrific job on that scene. There are a couple of shots of two little dots in the distance; it's the Indian running after Steiger. I don't know how Biroc caught that, but it was exactly what I wanted: you have to look for a moment before you notice them, because it's all vivid color, and then you see one speck chasing another speck.

China Gate

a. A lot of people liked *China Gate** and a lot of people didn't. I liked it. I liked the idea of doing Indo-China. I did a lot of research,

* *China Gate*. Lia (Angie Dickinson) agrees to lead a troop of French soldiers to a Communist Chinese ammunition depot so she can get special privileges for her son to be sent to America. The French troop is led by Brock (Gene Barry), Lia's estranged husband. Brock had deserted his family

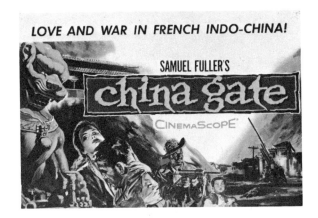

and I found out that the background of Indo-China was France's fault. So I put that in the prologue to the film. There was some resistance to my hitting it that hard. Now, I'll admit that the French were not the only heavies; so were the Dutch and the Japanese. But it was called French Indo-China, so we can't piddle—it wasn't called Dutch Indo-China or Alabama Indo-China. For I don't know how many hundreds of years, the French had it, and they milked it.

q. I like the scene where Angie Dickinson leaves Van Cleef and blows up the ammo dump, thus killing herself. It's done so quickly. She never stops to think, "What am I doing?" She just does it, because she has to. These types of decisions are found frequently in your films—for example, in *Underworld, U.S.A.,* when Tolly Devlin kills Boss Connors, and in *The Naked Kiss,* when Kelly kills Grant.

a. I think that's good drama. I think that's exciting. More important, if it's anything connected with death, it should be quick, unless you have a good dramatic reason for stalling—for example, in *Underworld,* when Robertson went to kill Paul Dubov. I didn't mind the stalling there, because first of all he's going to maneuver the death of this man; second, he's going to torture him; and third, he's not going to shoot him himself. But if Robertson were going to commit the act personally, I'd have him blow Dubov's head off as soon as he walks in the door. I don't mind stalling if there's an emotional reason for it. Otherwise, it's very hard for me to accept a lot of gibble-gabble before a shooting. Instead, I want *impact*.

When I told Angie to run through that cave, I conceived the whole thing as taking place in five seconds or less, from the beginning of the run to the blow-up. Because not only is time important, but if she *walked* there, we would fall into a dangerous category: now she's going to deliberate. She would be hesitant, and she shouldn't be hesitant. It's like a suicide. If you're going to kill yourself, kill yourself. Don't call the police and your mother and your father and your uncle.

One day, I'd like to do a picture about that. Somebody's about to kill himself, and he calls Joe—"Come on over!"—and he calls his girl. Well, she gets caught on the freeway in traffic, and it's too late by the time she gets there. I've always wanted to do something like that. But you hit on something that's very close to me: the *rapidity*. Didn't that scene shock you a little?

---

when their son was born with Oriental characteristics, inherited from Lia. When they reach the ammo dump, Lia dies to save the mission. Brock survives and finally accepts his son.

Forty Guns

a. I don't like the title *Forty Guns;* * it's meaningless to me. I was going to call it *Woman with a Whip.* Originally, Marilyn Monroe wanted to play the lead role. She liked the idea of this girl surrounded by all these men. I thought she was too young for what I wanted. I wanted a mother-sister flavor there.

The stuntmen refused to do the scene where the Stanwyck character

* *Forty Guns.* Griff Bonnell (Barry Sullivan) and his brother Wes (Gene Barry) ride into town and throw Brockie Drummond (John Ericson), a local troublemaker, into jail. Brockie's sister, Jessica (Barbara Stanwyck), comes with forty hired gunmen and frees Brockie. After Brockie kills Wes on Wes's wedding day, Griff confronts him. Using his sister's body as a shield, Brockie threatens Griff. Griff, ignoring his personal feelings toward Jessica, shoots both of them.

is dragged by a horse. They thought it was too dangerous. So Stanwyck said she'd do it, and she did it. We did it the first time, and I said, "I didn't like it. It was too far away from the camera truck. We're not getting what I want." So we tried it again, and I didn't like it. She made no complaint. We tried it a third time, and it was just the way I wanted it. She was quite bruised.

q.   There is a pervasive sense of death in the picture, connected with sexual acts specifically. The most striking example of this is the wedding scene, where the groom is shot and falls dead on his bride.

a.   You're right. I thought I would get a little touch of that in.

I liked the idea of the honeymoon bed being the grave. The only time he really got to touch her, he was dead.

I thought I would even contrast that scene a little bit, as far as sex was concerned, with the scene where the gunsmith's daughter measures Gene Barry for a weapon. I thought I'd have a little fun with sex, because the connotations were all there. I had a shot where he looks at the girl through a loose gun barrel, and as she walks, he pans with her, just like a camera. When I was in Paris, Godard told me he used that shot in *Breathless,* except that instead of a rifle, Belmondo rolls up a newspaper and follows Seberg when she's walking around his room. Godard said he took that from my film.

I couldn't use my original ending. I was asked to change it, and I changed it. The ending I originally shot was a powerful ending. I had Sullivan facing the killer, the young brother of Stanwyck. I had him grab Stanwyck and hold her in front of him. He knew he had Sullivan in a spot. I had him defy Sullivan. And Sullivan kills Stanwyck. Then he kills the boy and walks away. That was the end of the picture.

I had to put in that line where Sullivan says that he aimed the bullet so that it wouldn't kill Stanwyck. She's alive in the end, and they're happy. I didn't like that ending. A lot of people liked it, because they like to see the boy and the girl get together. I don't think that's important. I think it's much more dramatic the other way, because Sullivan has to blow his top. That's why he hasn't used a gun in ten years. But the moment he squeezes that trigger, he's a different man. He's an executioner, and he kills anything in front of him.

It's a rough ending. I've seen so many pictures, from *High Noon* back, where the heavy grabs the girl and holds her in front of him, putting the hero in a hell of an embarrassing situation. Always, at the last minute, she pushes him away, and the hero kills him. I don't like that in any Western. It doesn't make sense. That's why I wanted Sullivan not only to shoot Stanwyck, which the studio thought was enough, but to kill her.

Verboten

q. *Verboten** seems to be your most chaotic film. Every scene was done in a different style. For example, documentary footage was intercut with a street set, and film-clip montages intermingled with long-takes. What linked these scenes was that nearly every one dealt with a form of hysteria.

a. I'm very glad that you brought that up. I used the contrasts in shooting to help maintain chaos, because I'm very touchy about that subject, about post-war in Germany.

I had a very good ending, but I was forced to change it. I had the

* *Verboten.* Sergeant Brent (James Best) is the lone survivor of a Nazi ambush. Helga Schiller (Susan Cummings) takes him in and cares for his wounds. He falls in love with her and marries her. However, Helga is still a Nazi, and her old boyfriend, Bruno Eckart (Tom Pittman), is the leader of the German youth movement. Brent discovers that Helga's brother is involved in the neo-Nazi group, and then he discovers the whole situation. All chaos breaks loose.

American soldier shot at the end. I had him killed by an M.P., another American soldier, who saw this fellow walking around by the fire and shot him because he was dressed as a civilian. The other soldiers come over and say, "Who is it?" The M.P. turns the body over with his foot, and he says, "Ah hell, another Kraut." Not that I want every hero to die. In this case, I thought it would give me more impact.

But I'm very close to the subject of *Verboten*. During the war we had a lot of arguments over whether there is a difference between a German and a Nazi. With the exception of one experience I had, I did not meet a single German, from the day we invaded Germany to the end of the war in Czechoslovakia, who said he was a Nazi. The one exception was a fifteen- or sixteen-year-old girl in a little town outside of Aachen. I was on a patrol with several men, and we asked her for water. She told us to get our asses away from there. We even tried to impress on her that behind us was the First U.S. Infantry Division of 12,000 men. It meant nothing to her. That's the only German I ever met who told us she was a Nazi and told us to go to hell. I'll never forget that. Everyone else said, "I don't know what's going on." Just like the Southerner in *Run of the Arrow*. You know; it's always the other fellow.

I was very touchy about that. I took a lot of footage during the war. Not just good stuff. Great stuff. My stuff. Stuff you don't see in the Army Pictorial Service films.

The last battle of World War II was in Falkenow, Czechoslovakia. The town was near a concentration camp. It was a camp for Russian soldiers, but many Americans were in it. They were mostly dying of TB. Dogtags had been removed, so we couldn't tell which corpses were Americans and which were not.

The company commander went into the little town of Falkenow with a group of men. He stopped people on the street and asked them, "What about the camp? How do they treat them?" They said, "We don't know anything about the camp." He said, "Give 'em a shovel!"

He grabbed a whole group of people—Germans—and marched them right into the camp. He made them take the dead, line them up, row after row after row, dress them, put them in carts, lead the carts through the town, and then bury them.

I have all that on film. Rough! Little things in there: They're throwing dirt down in the grave, and the face of a corpse is uncovered. These Hitler Jugen kids have to climb down, cover the face with a handkerchief, and then continue with the burial. Rough stuff! The dead are being carted through the town, and a little boy runs out with a toy rifle. He doesn't know a funeral's going on. He goes bang-bang-bang-bang at the corpses with his rifle. I have it all on film.

So I'm touchy about that subject to the point where, in *Verboten,* I had to bring it out. Maybe that's why it's so chaotic.

q. Another way this chaos asserts itself is that the whole neo-Nazi situation doesn't even seem political.

a. There was no politics. Frustration, hunger, defeat, and wild kids, really wild kids: that's what it was like in Germany at the time. I didn't think it was right to go into political haranguing.

q. Why did you use Wagner and Beethoven so much on the soundtrack?

a. Well, that's à propos! In the beginning of the picture, I tried a ballet. I did it to music. I wanted Jimmy Best's movements to match the music. I yelled out the music and the directions to him: [Beethoven's Fifth] Bom-bom-bom-bom—"Move!"—Bom-bom-bom-bom—"Move over there!" Then, when we hit the Martin Luther Platz, and we hit the Germans, I go right to Wagner!

To me, Beethoven and Wagner—politically, spiritually, and musically—conflicted. That's why I was very wrought up with that. The rise of Hitler was told through Wagner: [Hums Wagner, progressively getting louder]. That's the way Hitler did it. He started with one man, and then there were two. That's why I used the music a hell of a lot. And then it's great for the ending. Jesus Christ! Wagner and fire and blond boys and horses! Good God, how can you go wrong with that?

q. The destructive forces in the film seemed to be running out of control.

a. Right. I tried especially to personify that in one scene, where the young German leader is told by another neo-Nazi, "We can't blow up these trucks because they're carrying medicine to the people. Now,

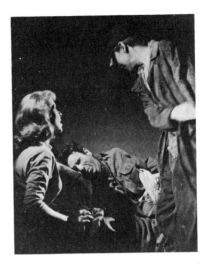

we'll fight the damn Americans, and we'll lie and cheat and steal and kill. We'll do anything for you, but we need the medicine for the people." The leader says, "Oh, the hell with them." The other guy says, "But these are Germans!" And the leader says, "THE HELL WITH THEM!"

That's why, in *Verboten,* I wanted to get the feeling of . . . you used the word chaos, which is good. I wanted to get the feeling of animal fury and viciousness.

The Crimson Kimono

a.　One of the oldest expressions in sex is "Let's change our luck." That means, "Let's go and get a colored girl." I thought it would be a good effect if I reversed the whole thing, so that when the white girl falls in love with the Japanese fellow, he says, "Now wait a minute. I want to make sure you really love me. I have a funny feeling that, just like the whites change their luck with a Negro, you're getting a kick out of finding out what it's like to get laid by an Oriental." I don't know why, but I left out that line of dialogue. I don't know if the idea came across. One day, I'll hit it. At one time, I even planned on using that line of dialogue in *Run of the Arrow.* I wanted to have the Indian girl think, "What is it like to lay a white man?" But anyway, that idea got me started on *Kimono*.*

The other thing that interested me in *Kimono* was to do the story of a white man, a white girl, and a Japanese, and when the two men fall in love with her, she picks the Japanese fellow. I thought the end of the picture was very honest. I hate phony, lying losers. I hate scenes, and I've seen them a thousand times, where one fellow loses the girl to another guy, and the loser says, "Well, we'll still be friends. Don't worry." No! Not in my film. He didn't give a damn whether the guy was yellow or white. He was angry because the guy stole his girl. And he stayed angry.

Another thing I wanted to bring out was that the bigot in the film was the Japanese. Not the white guy. The Japanese guy was acting like a white racist.

q. I like the note of contrasting delicacy in the ending. The killer is getting gunned down in the street, while all around are people in beautiful costumes with little jingling ornaments.

a. There's another place that I used music to establish contrast. Several bands are in that celebration at the end. One plays classical

music, one plays Japanese music, one plays hot music, and so on. Whenever I cut from the killer to the pursuer, the music changed. That gave me the discordant and chaotic note I wanted.

There's a highly experimental flavor to that picture. The whole thing was shot downtown in Little Tokyo. Since I was shooting a lot of street stuff at night with hidden cameras, I had to use a very fast, sensitive film. I couldn't use any lighting.

The opening scene was the most difficult I've ever had to do (and I've shot scenes with a thousand men in *Merrill's Marauders*). I hid three cameras, one on a roof, one in a truck, and another in a car. When the girl fell, at my gunshot, she fell in the middle of the street in traffic. We didn't stage it. That was real traffic. If some idiot had pulled out all of a sudden, the girl would have gotten it. Most dangerous scene I've ever shot.

I also discovered something very interesting in that scene: you *must* stage things. I learned that lesson. I had a tall, blond half-naked girl running down the street. All hidden cameras. She passed two sailors. They didn't pay any attention. She passed men who were walking down the street. Nobody paid attention. I have this on film. Terrible, terrible. Then I shot the gun. Nobody did anything. But when she fell, some stupid son of a bitch in a barber shop called the cops. We got her into the truck immediately, and we all disappeared. A big mob gathered. They were all saying, "What body? What body?" We wanted to go back to shoot a close-up. We had to wait till 2:30 in the morning until the street was cleared.

* *The Crimson Kimono.* Sugar Torch, a striptease, is shot down in a Los Angeles street. Joe Kojaku (James Shigeta) and Charlie Bancroft (Glenn Corbett), war buddies now turned policemen, are assigned to the case. Their only lead is Christine Downes (Victoria Shaw), who draws a picture of the killer. Charlie falls in love with Christine, but she and Joe fall in love. Suffering from a reverse racism, Joe resents his own feelings toward the girl, and he is convinced that Charlie does not approve of an Oriental falling in love with a white girl. The murderer is finally apprehended at a celebration in Little Tokyo. Joe realizes his foolishness, but Charlie is still left without his girl.

Underworld, U.S.A.

a. I figured I'd do *Monte Cristo*; I'd do Dumas. With one exception: instead of getting even with the guys personally, he uses the Law to knock off the people he doesn't like. I thought that was a pretty good approach to the story.

q. A theme of cleanliness runs through *Underworld, U.S.A.** It starts with Cliff Robertson sterilizing instruments in a prison hospital and ends when, as he's dying, he stumbles over a trashcan which says "Keep Your City Clean." Why did you use this?

* *Underworld, U.S.A.* When he was a child, Tolly Devlin (Cliff Robertson), now a petty safecracker, saw four shadows on a wall beat and kill his father. He devotes his life to tracking down the murderers. In a prison hospital, one of them divulges the names of the others as he dies. They are Gunther (Gerald Milton), Gela (Paul Dubov), and Smith (Allan Gruener), top men in a huge crime syndicate known as Underworld, U.S.A., which is run under the business front of National Projects by Earl "Boss" Connors (Robert Emhardt). Devlin infiltrates the organization and uses the Law to dispose of all three men. Having accomplished his purpose, he seeks to withdraw and marry Cuddles (Dolores Dorn), a prostitute he is using as a witness against Smith. However, by this time, he is too deeply entangled in Underworld, U.S.A., and

a. Again, I wanted contrast. In addition to sterilizing utensils, I told Robertson to put the bandages on the man very gently, very precisely, like a surgeon. I wanted to get that effect: he's clean about those bandages even though he's double-crossing the man he's putting them on.

I also tried to get a contrast wherever I could between the cleanliness of the head of National Projects and the discussion he's carrying on about narcotics and prostitution and murder. That's why I picked the swimming pool location. I wanted that hollow, clean atmosphere

you get around a swimming pool. It's too bad we can't have smell in motion pictures, because there's an antiseptic smell around a pool, like in a gym. I thought that the cleanest thing in the world is a pool. So I had this crime organization hold their meetings there, rather than in the pompous office or the pool hall or the dingy little room where gangsters usually hang out. I wanted to get that contrast to what they're talking about: it's so vile and low.

q. Another motif was the emphasis on Robertson's clenched fist. It had such double-edged, perverse connotations. Again, it was more than an ordinary symbol, because it was constantly changing. For

he must kill Connors to free himself. In the struggle Tolly is shot. He dies in the same alley in which his father was murdered.

example, there was a great dissolve from his fist clenched in anger at the detention home to his fist clenched while he's picking a safe.

a. The symbol of the fist is his spite against society. Pictorially and emotionally, it tells a story. It's his fight. He's fighting all the time. I also wanted its anger. Tremendous anger. The fist represented his dialogue to the cop when he was a boy. He said, "I'll get 'em!"

The other connotations you mentioned are there also. When he was a boy, and he rifled the drunk, I wanted the light to hit his hand, his fist. It didn't quite come off, because I mainly wanted that scene to be moody and dark. I didn't want an obvious light, because then it would have looked stagey.

I like the sex in the picture between Robertson and Dolores Dorn.

You know, he laughs at her and says, "Me? Marry a hooker?" Then, when he changes his mind, I wanted to get it so lackadaisical. I wanted an affrontery to human feelings. He says, "Oh, all right. A guy needs a partner. O.K., we'll get married." I thought that *that* showed you the character of the fist more than if I had shown an emotional thing there.

q. Why did you depict National Projects, the front for Underworld, U.S.A., as such a typical business organization, with adding machines and bankers and everything?

a. It's all done mechanically, almost like robots, like computer systems. I don't doubt that crime today is governed by computers. If I were to make that picture today, I'd show nothing but twenty machines. No people, just all the machines. I wanted to get that flavor of mechanization in the picture.

q. It seemed to be that crime was defined in the film as lack of emotion. Underworld, U.S.A., was lack of emotion.

a. Yes. And also a facade of good citizenship. Remember that Boss Connors said, "We'll always win. All we have to do is pay a little taxes, go to church, send a couple of kids through school, set up a few charities on the side. We'll win. We always have. We always will."

When I shot the bookkeeping and the adding machines and all

that, I tried to show the man's hand in the foreground hitting the keys very fast. That, to me, was Underworld, U.S.A., what he was doing: tic-tic-tic-tic bing-bing tic-tic-tic-tic. It never stopped.

q. The coldness of the organization is particularly well reflected in the Richard Rust character, the paid killer. He commits his murders totally without commitment, almost casually.

a. Now there's an honest character! He's not a psychotic; there's nothing insane about him. He just has a job. He certainly isn't interested in killing that little kid. There's no vengeance in it. There's no emotion in the man at all. That's what finally terrorizes Robertson—the way Rust says, "We have to wipe out this girl. If you do a good job, it'll get you in with the Boss." The only emotion he has is that it will get him in with the Boss. To knock off a girl means nothing to him.

I didn't want Rust to do anything that deviated from the character of a professional killer, except one thing. I told him, "When you're getting ready to kill somebody, put on your dark glasses. Then we'll never know whether or not you want to see anything, or whether or not you're feeling anything." You see, I wanted to keep away from emotion. I didn't want a character like in the old gangster pictures: he likes his mother, he supports his brother, he has a little dog, he feeds goldfish. I didn't want that.

q. When the policeman is instructing his men how the underworld operates, it's done in the same monotone, matter-of-fact manner as when Connors instructs his criminals.

a. You got the balance there? While the lawman is telling them all about National Projects, a phone in the background rings. He just glances for a second and points, and someone picks up the phone. The camera is moving in on him all this time. He keeps on talking; the fluidity of his speech is never interfered with.

I did the same thing with Connors, the heavy. When he's talking in that private home, the phone rings, and he just points. This is what I wanted to bring out: they are both the same man. They're worried. They're tired. They're concentrating on what they're saying. They have listeners who will not object, and no matter what happens outside that little realm of their thinking, someone else has to take care of it.

q. You use newspapers in a lot of your films, and I particularly liked their use in this one. It seemed to me that you set up a deliberate contrast between witnessing the terrifying corruption of Underworld, U.S.A., such as the murder of the little girl, and then seeing these things on the printed page, completely depersonalized.

a. I agree with you. Usually, newspapers are overdone in movies. But I don't mind showing something and then showing a contrast of it in the press. I feel the same way about flashbacks. Unless the flashback has nothing to do with the actual situation, I don't like it. Let me give you an example of what I mean. The character says, "When I was a little girl, my mother used to give me a piece of candy." As she's saying that, you flashback: the mother's beating the hell out of her. I don't mind that kind of flashback. But if you actually show the mother giving her candy, I can't take that. That's the way I feel about using a newspaper.

q. Robertson is the only one in the film who acts on personal grounds. He wasn't motivated by a newspaper story; he actually witnessed his father's murder.

a. I used the same thing in *Pickup on South Street*. This is human nature: In *Pickup,* Widmark didn't care about anything. Didn't care! But when he found out that someone took a beating for him, that someone was physically hurt who was tied up with him, he said, "O.K. That's it," and he went right after the enemy.

The same with Robertson. He didn't give a damn. But since he's committed himself, on his level, to a partner, and since now he's assigned to kill this partner, then he has to go after Connors. Because if Rust doesn't kill her, someone else will.

It's a theme I like in a picture. I never like a man to do something heroic for any chauvinistic or false premise other than emotional, personal necessity. If a newspaper says, "GREAT HERO SAVES 12,000 PEOPLE FROM BEING BOMBED IN A STADIUM," we know he didn't save 12,000 people. He saved *one*. That's what I'm trying to bring out.

Merrill's Marauders

q. The theme of the fighter is carried over into your next picture, *Merrill's Marauders.** It's summed up when Merrill says, "As long as you can take another step, you can fight."

a. That's the whole story. In *Merrill's Marauders,* the theme that I thought would be very, very strong is not just of a man saying, "You do what I do"—which is epitomized by his saying, "You put one foot forward; you take another step," and so on. That's only fifty per cent. I wanted to go beyond that. I wanted to show that when he says, "You do what I do," that means, "When I die, you die." That's the main thing I wanted to bring out. That's the Big Baby.

Quite a lot of the picture was improvised, since we shot the whole thing on location. When we were shooting in this little village in the

* *Merrill's Marauders.* General Frank Merrill (Jeff Chandler) agrees to lead his troops to make a final stand at Myitkyina, North Burma. After several ambushes, plagues of typhoid fever, and weeks without supplies, the troops refuse to go on to their final destination, the airfield. Merrill, on the verge of a heart attack, walks through his ragged troops and tells them, "As long as you can take another step, you can fight." He then falls over dead. Inspired, his soldiers begin to rise and move on.

Philippines, I noticed a little boy who kept following me. So I told Claude Akins, one of my actors, "I have an idea." This was all improvised, and it turned out very nicely: The Marauders came into this town. They're resting; they're exhausted; they're hungry, but they're too tired to eat. The little boy comes up and looks at Akins' beard. When he started to scratch the beard, that gave me another idea: feeding. So this old woman comes over and offers rice to an American soldier—who, as you know, is the best-fed soldier in the world. When Akins realizes the idiocy and the stupidity, the irony and the shame, that he, a big, burly, well-fed man, is being fed by this scrawny old woman, he starts to cry. That, to me, is more important than anything else in the picture. It affected me, because I know how it is to take food.

    q.   Was the battle among the concrete blocks also improvised?

    a.   There used to be several tanks—I think they were fuel tanks—supported on these big triangular stones. During the war, the tanks were blown up. The stones remained. When I saw those stones, I immediately got the idea for that battle scene. They reminded me of the dragons' teeth of the Siegfried Line in Germany. We fought like that in the dragons' teeth. That's chaos again.

    The producers took out a couple of things I wanted in that scene. I wanted to get an effect of people shooting blindly, of Americans shooting other Americans. Because it's panic! The whole thing is panic. But I had to draw the line. After all, I was told, it's a war picture. You're going to be showing it to mothers and fathers, and they're going to say, "What is this? It's enough that if our boy is shot, he's killed by an enemy. Does it have to be his own friend who shoots him?" Yes! It does. That's what happens.

    My favorite scene in the picture is when the officer climbs on top of the stones after the battle. I make a 360-degree turn with him as he's looking at the dead, and he can't distinguish between the Americans and the enemy. They're all mixed up. That's what I'd like to hit on more than anything else. If people like war, they should just take a look when the fighting's all over.

    The scene of the night fight was done without any lights. The only lights we had were from the explosions. I had thirty-six explosions for the first shot. The first take was ruined, because the explosions knocked the camera right down.

q. The film ended strangely, before it was resolved.

a. The ending was an abortion. I was originally going to end with a sequence of the airfield being taken. We were going to go out with a lot of action. They decided not to shoot it for two reasons, both of them money. So I said, "O.K. All we can do is end it where they're walking away and then fade out." Someone went ahead and put not only a narration there but also a stock shot of soldiers marching. Well, that was their business. My business was the thrill I got out of a review by a Vancouver critic. He loved the picture. He said that the entire film looked like a documentary, and that the only thing that looked Hollywood was the stock shot at the end! Is that a hell of a review?

Shock Corridor

a. Originally, I don't know how many years ago, I wanted to do a film exposing conditions in the mental hospitals of the United States. Then I decided to do it as a fiction piece instead of a documentary exposé. I said, "The hell with it! I can pull a Nellie Bly!" Nellie Bly, you know, impersonated a nut for a while in the Wards Island insane asylum many years ago. So I thought I'd dramatize a fellow who goes into an asylum to crack a murder and winds up insane. I'm glad I didn't make it when I originally intended to. Even if it had been the same

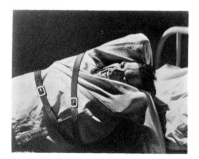

story, it wouldn't have had the same up-to-date flavor: the combination Oppenheimer-Einstein-Teller, the tremendous [James] Meredith situation, and the turncoats of Korea. So I put that all together, and I modernized it, and that was *Shock Corridor.**

I enjoyed making that picture. I liked the idea of using color before a man became lucid. When he's insane, and he's thinking of something, once we see color, we know that immediately after that he'll be rational for a few minutes, because he's remembering. So each one had his own little color. For the Southern soldier, I used Japan. When I went location-hunting for *House of Bamboo,* I shot a hell of a lot of stuff with my own camera. That's what I used for his nightmare. I have about 8,000 feet of film on the Mato Grosso. I went there once looking for locations, and I lived with the Kataja Indian tribe for six or seven weeks. I used that for the Negro's nightmare. In Peter Breck's nightmare at the end, the waterfall coming down is part of the Iguazu Falls in the Mato Grosso. I shot all of this in Cinemascope and 16mm. I didn't have it unsqueezed. All I did was blow it up to 35mm. So there it was, giving a weird effect without my doing anything.

q. Was there any particular reason why Dr. Boden didn't have a visual nightmare, but an aural one?

a. Oh, that was intentional. I don't know why, but I get a certain feeling when I think of a laboratory, Oppenheimer and all that. I see big buildings and big rooms—hollow chambers—little holes—and voices coming out. I feel that. You know: "Dr. So-and-so, will you please report to so-and-so." I don't see phones. I see nothing but an intercom. A big,

---

* *Shock Corridor.* Johnny Barrett (Peter Breck), a reporter, seeks the Pulitzer prize. His plan is to pose as an inmate in a mental hospital and solve a murder that had been committed there. He gleans information from three inmates: Stuart (James Best), a deserter from the Korean War, Trent (Hari Rhodes), who was unsuccessful as the first Negro student in a Southern college, and Boden (Gene Evans), a former nuclear scientist who now has the mind of a child. By the time Barrett uncovers the murderer, the pressures of his impersonation have driven him insane, and the final shots find him joining the permanent inhabitants of Shock Corridor.

weird, almost science-fiction flavor—that's what I wanted to get. I also wanted one thing that sets Boden apart from the others: voices and, more importantly, the coldness of it.

I have a sequence in the film of Constance Towers doing a strip that I should have cut out. It's too long. But I left it in, like an idiot. I wanted to do a strip without any cuts, without an audience, and without applause. It didn't belong. I should have cut out everything but the end of the strip.

q. The pattern of these witnesses' insanity is very interesting. They're all the opposite of what they used to be: The Negro imagines

he's the leader of the KKK. Boden, the great scientific genius, has the mind of a five-year-old. The deserter imagines he's a great soldier, J.E.B. Stuart. When the reporter goes insane, he follows the same pattern. Being involved with communication, newspapers, it's fitting that he should lose his voice.

a. That's the whole point. The voluble man loses his voice. That was the only way I could get a contrast for him. I racked my brain for that.

Again, I tried to get as much contrast as I could. To me, that's movies. I thought the sound trick I used when Pagliacci is conducting the imaginary music was effective. We hear this tremendous orchestra playing until the camera gets off of his face. Then the music stops. I thought that was a good contrast for pointing up the absolute quietness of the place.

I don't know if you heard the dialogue there, where Pagliacci tells the young reporter how he sang his wife to death. Now, generally these men despise anything physical. That's why he says, in his lucid moment, "Somebody killed Sloane in the kitchen . . . and with a *knife!*" That, to me, is important. A mentally sick person, no matter how violent he is, despises violence. Isn't that interesting? I don't know enough about that.

I once visited a mental ward in New York. I went with a young cop, a rookie, who thought he'd pull a fast one on me. When we were in this ward, he closed the door, barred it, to lock me in. But he misjudged. There were so many barred doors that he locked himself in. He thought it was the other way around. Doors going this way, that way—it was weird! I began to laugh. I was a kid; I was eighteen. Then he said, "Now you go over there, and you get the key." He whispered this very softly, because he didn't want anyone to hear. And I said, "WHAT DID YOU SAY? YOU WANT A KEY TO GET OUT?" Oh, I loved that scene. I loved it.

q. Of course, the great tour de force is the thunderstorm scene in the corridor. Could you discuss how you shot it?

a. Of course! I thought it would be fresh to show a thunderstorm just as if it happened right here in this room. I needed really a lot of water. Now, you must realize this was a dangerous situation, because there was no outlet for the water on this particular sound stage. You have to have a tank under the floor for the drainage. Otherwise, you can ruin a lot of equipment.

We didn't have any of these things, but I did it anyway, because I knew it was going to be the last day of shooting. I had to get what I wanted on the first take. To be very careful about it, I had a regular camera on Breck and a second camera above that one, tipped down and shooting in close-up. I didn't want to have to stop; I couldn't afford

the time. I had everything ready for me. In other words, the door was open, and my car was running. I had to make a hasty exit, since I'm chicken. I didn't want to be around when the studio manager came in and started asking a lot of questions. As Breck screamed, I waited twenty seconds. I wanted the biggest scream I could get. Then, I said, "Forget it!" and I ran out. I never went back—to the studio or the set.

I don't say "Cut!"; I say "Forget it!" at the end of a scene. That means to really forget that scene. Everybody, cast and crew, just forget it. Physically and mentally, forget it; we're on something else now. "Cut!" always makes me think of the holy rites of circumcision. I don't know why, but it always does.

q. How do you evaluate Dr. Cristo's character? Do you find him particularly sympathetic or noteworthy?

a. No. To me, Dr. Cristo is a symbol of all officials in a hospital. I dramatized him as being understanding *until* he becomes slightly suspicious.

q. Cristo says, "You can't tamper with the mind," and implies that this is why the reporter went insane. But were you trying to say more than that: that everyone has this insanity inside of him?

a. Sure. I should have emphasized that even more strongly in the film. I should have made it clearer that for the reporter to want to do this, to volunteer to be accepted as an inmate, he had to be a little crazy in the first place.

Every one of us naturally has an inclination to yell or go crazy or break things. Even if you don't think that's a form of insanity, I do. They say it's an outlet. It's not. A fellow gets sore, and he slams the door. Why the hell is this? It's not even childish; it's being insane. When inmates go around from one room to another slamming doors, people say, "Look at them. They're crazy." When we do it, we say we have a reason: we're angry. Well, we don't know what's going on in their minds: they're angry every minute. Just angry! So they're slamming doors every minute.

I'm positive that, next to death, insanity is one of the most interesting subjects for me. I mean, I'm intrigued by it. If you made a picture

about insane people, I'd love to see it, no matter what. I have another story on a mental hospital that I'm going to do some day.

The Naked Kiss

q.   I think that *The Naked Kiss** is in many ways more "shocking" than *Shock Corridor*.

a.   It is.

q.   In fact, I would say that it's the most shocking film you've made. It seemed that you deliberately went to lengths to get a reaction

---

* *The Naked Kiss*. Kelly (Constance Towers), a prostitute, arrives in a small town. After sleeping with the police chief (Anthony Eisley), she is promptly directed across the river to the local bordello. She somehow gets the directions mixed up, and winds up leading a respectable life. She falls in love with Grant (Michael Dante), the millionaire civic leader, and becomes engaged to him, although she withdraws, oddly enough, from his first kiss. The day before their marriage, she finds him molesting a child. The kiss she had received from him is known in prostitutes' parlance as a "Naked Kiss": the kiss of a pervert. Her dreams shattered, she bludgeons him to death with a telephone receiver. She is arraigned for murder, and the town refuses to believe the truth about Grant. Eventually, the child is found, and Kelly is exonerated. She leaves town and goes back to being a prostitute.

from the audience, especially when you pull the rug out from under everything in the child-molesting scene.

a.   In *Naked Kiss* I maintained that (I tried to get this in *Pickup,* too) no matter how low someone is, in the depths of his or her profession, there's someone lower. Then, no matter how low that person is, when he finds someone lower, he's shocked, he's hurt. The hookers, who resent that they are resented by the country club set, would resent someone lower than they are. Do you understand? That's the first thing I wanted to bring out.

I wanted to bring something else out, but I don't know if I succeeded, because we were short on loot, the bastards. I had a scene where Constance Towers confronts the townspeople after they find out that she's innocent. First they were ready to lynch her, and now they want

vindication. She tells them to go to hell. I didn't shoot this scene—no money. She calls them hypocrites, which is all right, *but* the important thing is that she realizes how happy she was in her profession. She says, in effect, "What a thrill it is: when you get through laying any of those bastards, he pays you off and leaves. You don't have to listen to him or to his stories or to his lies, like I have to listen to your lies every day." That's what I wanted. Another thing I like about the picture, which maybe millions hated or thousands or two hundred that saw it, was the

idea of a girl going back to being a hooker. I just like it.

I thought it would be very effective if a girl kills a saint, and no one believes that the saint is really guilty of a horrible crime. That's the premise I wanted. How do I make this man saintly and canonize him? I make him the sweetest man in the world, with all sorts of charitable gadgets: hospitals, a town named after him, and so on.

So when I started the film as a shocker, the original impression I wanted was of a wonderful, almost dull, very, very ordinary love story: the poor girl from the wrong side of the tracks, the rich man who falls in love with her. Well, I hate those kinds of stories. So I knew I was going to have fun the minute she finds him molesting the child. Now, when you saw the picture, did that scene shock you?

q. To say the least.

a. Good. That's what I wanted. I don't mean that I wanted it to shock you content-wise; I wanted it to shock you story-wise.

A lot of people didn't like that picture. Certain friends of mine said, "Oh, why'd you have him try to lay a little girl?" I don't know, maybe they resented it because of some secret, hidden desire. What would you expect me to do? Suppose there's no child-molesting scene. I wouldn't have made the story. There is no story, in that case, as far as I'm concerned. I'm not interested in the girl from the wrong side of the tracks. They made those stories at Metro and Warners' for fifty years: She

goes to the right side, she meets the fellow, sometimes she finds out he's a nice guy, sometimes she finds out he's a phony, but there's always a happy ending.

I do know that when you have a movie like *The Naked Kiss,* and you use a star cast instead of unknowns like I used, the reaction is different. For example, I just saw a picture on television called *Suddenly Last Summer.* I know that if it had not been written by Tennessee Williams, and if Mankiewicz had used a couple of unknowns, and it was made for a couple of dollars, and it was shuffled out by someone like Allied Artists, you never would have heard of it. If you had heard of it, you would have said, "It's too despicable." I'm not complaining. I don't usually like to think of big names when I'm making a picture; I've made quite a number of films with unknowns. I just know that sometimes, with a delicate or shocking subject, you're better off using good old-fashioned Hollywood names.

I thought I had some good stuff in *Naked Kiss.* I liked the idea that the townspeople could not believe that their canonized leader could do anything wrong, when we knew differently. There's nothing unusual about that. To me, what was unusual was to show a woman who searches for some damn kind of happiness, a kind of security that she envies, that other women have, and when she finds it, it's all smashed and blasted.

I don't know why some people don't like it. I like *The Naked Kiss*. There are little things I probably should have done. When I say "little things," I mean story-wise, nothing else. Maybe the subject matter was too distasteful. I don't know. Was *Suddenly Last Summer* a very big hit?

q. Yes.

a. Well, there you are. Then I'm wrong. The subject matter was not too distasteful. Or else, maybe I didn't handle it subtly enough. I thought I handled it pretty well, because I got past the censors. They said, "How are you going to shoot the scene where she comes in and sees the little girl being molested?" I said, "We just go on faces. The little girl. The man. The older woman. Then the little girl just trotting out. That's all." I thought that worked.

q. The opening scene is astonishing, where Towers beats up the pimp as her wig is falling off. The viewer is assaulted before the credits even come on.

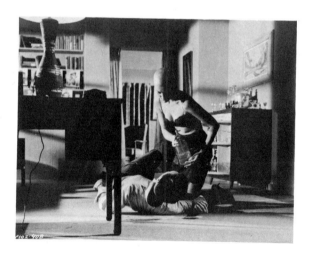

a. Did that surprise you, that beginning? There's no fade-in, you know. We open with a direct cut. In that scene, the actors utilized the camera. They held the camera; it was strapped on them. For the first shot, the pimp has the camera strapped on his chest. I say to Towers, "Hit the camera!" She hits the camera, the lens. Then I reverse it. I put the camera on her, and she whacks the hell out of him. I thought it was effective. She had a difficult time making herself up at the end of the scene, because she had to use the lens as a mirror. As the titles come on, she's looking into the lens.

q. There are many artistic references in the film, mostly connected with Grant, the millionaire. The most outstanding ones are to Beethoven.

a. Ah! First of all, I wanted to show that the millionaire's a very "nice" man; he likes to sit and listen to music, and all that stuff. The girl is very hungry for something like that. Beethoven is a symbol. It could have been any other composer or artist. I wanted to show a contrast between Grant and the cop, who says, "I don't know anything about Beethoven." I put in that line for a reason. I had to have a hook, so that when she meets the rich man, and he brings up a certain subject—

Beethoven, we would say, "Oh, my! This is wonderful. He likes what I like. But the cop doesn't." That's the primary reason I used that.

Second reason: I love Beethoven. I'd squeeze him in any place. I want to tell you a story. This actually happened. In the war, when we went into Bonn, Germany, we holed up in certain houses. I went into this one house with a man called Johnson, who was from Nashville, Tennessee. We slept there until morning. When the light came through the window, I looked up, and I saw manuscripts on the wall: Eroica, the Fifth, the Ninth, a sonata. Letters. Busts. Paintings. And it hit me. Naturally, this was the famous Beethoven museum. I woke up Johnson. He was terrified. He said, "What's the matter?!" I said, "Beethoven was here!" He said, "Who?" I said, "Beethoven!" And he said, "What outfit?" I said, "Johnson, you must have heard of Beethoven." I started to hum [Beethoven's Fifth], "Bom-bom-bom-bom. He wrote that." He said, "Oh! A songwriter!" I said, "Well, not exactly. He wrote music." Johnson said, "You mean like Irving Berlin! 'White Christmas'!" That's a true story.

I'm crazy about Beethoven as a *man*. I want to film his life someday. You see, he supported his nephew, went in hock for his nephew, who was never appreciative. I don't know if there's an afterlife, but if there is, I assure you, the first thing I'm going to do is look up Beethoven's nephew, and I'm going to kick the hell out of him! Because he made life *miserable* for this man. I'm going to kill him—again.

q. What were you intending with the imaginary trip to Venice during the big love scene?

a. I wanted that very badly for many reasons. First of all, I'm trying to sell him as a poetic, musical type—the fellow she wants so badly. She's never had anything like this before. The Venice scenes gave me a chance to show that pictorially.

But what I wanted more than anything else was to use that to build up to The Kiss, The Naked Kiss. I have him kiss her in the gondola, with the leaves falling. I cut on that position to them kissing on the couch. One more leaf falls. We'll never know whether that's in her mind or it really happened. The minute she kisses him, she draws away. He says, "What's the matter?" She says, "Nothing." That's when she should have said, "There's something wrong with you." But she didn't.

I had to have something highly molasses-like, even cornily romantic, in that scene. I couldn't just have them kissing on the couch. I had to have all that phony mood for one reason: I thought if I gave him an overload of gibble-gabble—about poets and painters and writers and musicians—we would understand why she doesn't object right then. I had to get a man who symbolized everything she was hungry for. I went overboard. I had to.

When she does find out this man's secret, and she realizes that he had given her a Naked Kiss, she's shocked, and he's shocked that she's shocked. Since she's a hooker, he thought that she would understand why he likes little girls. Why should she be surprised? He just hit the wrong girl. I thought that was good copy.

Shark

a. When I made *Shark** I had what I felt was a brainstorm: doing a story about four amoral characters. One is a scientist: no morals. One is the girl he's laying: no morals. One is the young hero: no morals. One is the cop: no morals. I thought it would be interesting to show not only a double-cross on a double-cross, but when we think we know who the heavy is, we find out that the real heavy behind it is the girl. She's the lowest. She does have a chance to get out of it alive, if she levels with the lead. But she doesn't. She is responsible for her own death. He lets her die. In other words, I tried something different there. They're in love and all that stuff, and I have the hero not only allow her to die, but he shrugs it off. I thought that was exciting.

I like the idea of a love affair where the man finds out the girl has used him. I gave her a great line of dialogue. In the last line of the picture—now I find out that the producers have put it in ahead, and it's no longer the last line—she says to him, "We're both a couple of bastards—only I'm a rich one." That's the whole flavor I wanted. I shot

* *Shark* was formerly titled *Twist of the Knife* and *Caine*.

some great stuff. For instance, when the boat is sinking at the end, he takes a lighted cigarette and throws it into the sea. I just stay on that cigarette. A fish sees it (the fish being a symbol of the shark), thinks it's something, and grabs it—pssshhht! [Sound of a cigarette being extinguished.] That's the end of the picture. Now I think they've cut it out. A lot of things like that were cut out.

As you know, I asked them to take my name off the damn thing, because I didn't like the cut I saw. I thought it was terrible. I told them I wanted to restore my original cut, or I'd try to get my name taken off it. They said they didn't know if they could get the film from Mexico. They couldn't locate it. It was such a confused state of affairs. Finally, I told them, "Don't bother me about it anymore." It may be the world's worst picture, or it may turn out to be a surprise to me. I don't know. I do know I had fun with the characters, because I went beyond the average switch of revealing the villain. I also didn't have a guy just letting a girl go off to jail; he lets her be eaten up by sharks. I've never seen anything like that in a picture before. Have you? That's my ending. That's what I shot.

The only reason I first called the picture *Caine* is that we went to a restaurant in Mexico where the service was bad. I got sore, and while I was getting sore, I felt like Cain, so I said, "Well, we'll call it *Caine*." That's all. Hell. I felt like hell. Then the producer saw a layout in *Life* magazine, some pictures of a guy being killed by a shark or something like that, and it said, "Shark." So they changed the title!

Well, that's the checkered career of an ex-copyboy. That's 30.

PROJECTS: PAST, PRESENT, AND FUTURE. In an article* titled "What Is a Film?," Fuller writes that he is obsessed by his work, that "art is a talent that seizes the creator . . . sometimes a blessing, sometimes a curse, but always a monster draining the artist." We present here several of Fuller's most cherished projects.

* *Cinema,* II, 2, July 1964, p. 22.

Flowers of Evil

Unrealized. Prepared for shooting in France in 1966. Abandoned when financing fell through.

They came to me with a very bad imitation of *Lysistrata*. I rewrote it completely. I changed the title, and I got the wonderful idea of casting a hand. I never saw anybody use that. I would have had a lot of try-outs write for me. I'd have just watched the hands until I found the right one. It's the hand of Baudelaire! The name of the picture would have been *Flowers of Evil,* not based on his poem, nothing to do with it, except that he created the title, and I wanted to give him the credit. So the picture would have opened with this hand writing the title and signing the name "Baudelaire."

I wrote a screenplay that I thought was way ahead of all these so-called science-fiction stories. This was science fiction, but it was beyond it. My ending had these two characters in space. The fellow cannot reach this girl; he cannot save her. He has to come back to earth. The last thing in the film is that she will revolve and revolve and revolve until she disintegrates. I thought that was a hell of an ending. Her voice gets smaller and smaller and weaker as she's yelling. That was it.

The Rifle

The movie would be made from a book about the Vietnam war, to be published in fall 1969.

Louis Sobol, the Broadway columnist and author of *The Longest Street,* was my editor and published the book. He was my colleague in the early days on the New York *Evening Graphic.* I plan to make this movie sometime in late 1969 or early part of 1970, hopefully to shoot it in Asia. I will use my wife, Christa Lang, as the insane nun in the story. Aside from the Colonel, my plan is to use unknown actors to portray the 14-year-old North Vietnamese boy who is a professional killer; a soldier blood thief who keeps himself alive stealing blood from the other wounded; a draft-card burner who winds up in an infantry platoon; a Negro turncoat of the Korean police action who finds life miserable in Watts

Fuller with his wife, Christa Lang.

and seeks liberation of being a "token" by rejoining the Army to fight in Vietnam.

The Eccentrics

Script completed. May be shot in Spain in summer 1969.

I have a yarn about this famous woman writer who gathers the hippies around her because she's going to do a book about them. See, she has such an imagination that we always see her imagination. It's not a question of trick photography. She can be talking to somebody, and when we see something, that means she's thinking of a story. I can go wild on this.

To give you an example: I open up the picture with an eagle flying. A feather falls. I follow the feather. It lands. A man picks up the feather. I pull back: he's a hunter. He makes an arrow. He keeps looking at the eagle. Then he shoots the arrow. The arrow, with that same feather, kills the eagle. I cut, and we are zooming up, from twelve or fifteen stories below, to a woman in a white Nehru coat and red boots standing on the edge of the roof. Behind her is a hippie, beard and beads and all that. She looks down, and she sees traffic. She looks up, and she says something about an eagle. He says, "Did you write it?" She says, "No. Aesop wrote it." "What happened to him?" "His fans killed him," she says. That's the story of *The Eccentrics*. Then she looks down again, and there's an ocean. She jumps, and I cut to her running down the stairs. In the middle of the stairs is a boat with the drunken Rimbaud in it. She throws the boat over and watches him crash with the boat. This is the seventh-story stairwell. Now she runs down the street, and there are 150 typewriters on the ground. Pages of paper are following her. She goes back to her houseboat. She jumps in the water, and she's yelling for help. She wakes up, and the guy she's keeping is watching her. She says, "I had a little dream. A couple of things I'm working on." We're just seeing her mind.

The Lusty Days

Future. Script completed.

This is a Civil War yarn. It's about a guy who uses a girl's ass to get votes for Lincoln. In most pictures, when you see Lincoln, you know, he's huddled up in a rocking chair with a shawl around him and he's wearing spectacles and all that. That's not my Lincoln. My Lincoln would go out himself with a carpetbag to collect votes if he had to. Because that's the way politics was in those days. That's the story of *The Lusty Days*.

Balzac

Future. Would be shot in France.

It's got nothing to do with him as a writer. In other words, we'll know he's a writer, and that's all. I'm interested in him as a human being. It's a very sexy story. Highly sexy. The sex just poured out of this man. It's not just good; it's wonderful.

Rimbaud

Future. Would be shot in France.

This is the key scene I want in his life. I want to dramatize it, because I think it's so great: Just picture a young boy, Rimbaud, whose mother is very worried because he is getting fucked by an older homo.

Now the older homo has a wife. The mother of the young man and the wife of the older writer get together in Paris, and they say, "We've got to do something about this." So they take a train, and they go to Holland. They go to this little rooming house. They go up to the door, and they know that inside that room the son and the husband are getting boffed. Who knocks on the door? That's their number one problem. When they do knock on the door, who is the one who's going to speak? And then I'm going to have a sequence that'll be so shocking! They're going to find these two guys in bed. They know that. They go in anyway. They were both so reluctant, and now the two guys are sore as hell at them, especially the older one: "How can you do this? There are no manners anymore! Nothing! You could have knocked! You could have waited!" I want to get the funniest goddamned scene. Isn't that an unusual flavor?

The Big Red One

Future. Fuller's most cherished project. A treatment of the progress of the First Infantry Division in World War II. To be realized as both a film and a novel.

My big love is *The Big Red One*. I think I've been working on it since the Second Battle of Bull Run. That's how long it seems. I want

Fuller (asleep on the left) during World War II. Scene to be re-enacted in The Big Red One.

to shoot in seven countries. Seven countries, seven women, five men: that's the whole story. It's a three-hour show. I don't think that's asking too much, because it starts out in Africa and ends up in Czechoslovakia. It shows the beginning of a war. This is where my story begins: Who fires the first shot? How does a war actually, physically start? War may be declared, but somebody has to kill somebody before it can begin. I go to the very last day of the war. This one man does not know the war is over. What happens to him is the really important thing in the story, because the verb "kill" becomes "murder."

FILMOGRAPHY

Born August 12, 1912 in Worcester, Massachusetts. In addition to his own films, Fuller worked on the scripts of the following productions: *Hats Off* (Boris Petroff, 1936), *It Happened in Hollywood* (Harry Lachman, 1937), *Gangs of New York* (James Cruze, 1938), *Shockproof* (Douglas Sirk, 1948), *The Command* (David Butler, 1954). Fuller supplied story ideas for the following films: *Adventure in Sahara* (D. Ross Lederman, 1938), *Federal Manhunt* (Nick Grinde, 1938), *Bowery Boy* (William Morgan, 1940), *Confirm or Deny* (Archie Mayo, 1941), *Power of the Press* (Lew Landers, 1943), *Gangs of the Waterfront* (George Blair, 1945), *The Tanks Are Coming* (Lewis Seiler, 1951). *Scandal Sheet* (Phil Karlson, 1952) is based on the novel by Fuller called *The Dark Page*.

I Shot Jesse James—1949 (81 minutes)
Producer: Robert L. Lippert. *Script:* Samuel Fuller. *Photography:* Ernest Miller. *Cast:* John Ireland (Robert Ford), Preston Foster (John Kelley), Barbara Britten (Cynthy Waters), Reed Hadley (Jesse James).

The Baron of Arizona—1950 (93 minutes)
Producer: Carl K. Hittelman (Lippert Productions). *Script:* Samuel Fuller. *Photography:* James Wong Howe. *Cast:* Vincent Price (James Addison Reavis), Ellen Drew (Sofia Peralta Reavis), Beulah Bondi

(Loma Morales), Vladimir Sokoloff (Pepito Alvarez), Reed Hadley (John Griff), Karen Kester (Sofia as a child).

James Addison Reavis (Vincent Price) painstakingly plans the biggest swindle in history. He selects a young Spanish-American girl (Ellen Drew) and elaborately forges documents which establish her as the heiress of a Spanish land grant encompassing all of Arizona. He marries her and seeks ratification of his title as the Baron of Arizona. The outraged citizens of the state attempt to lynch him, but he is saved by his wife, who has grown to love him. By this time, his hoax has been uncovered by government agents. After serving a jail sentence, Reavis finds his wife waiting for him outside the prison walls.

Fuller: What I was interested in was a man with a child. When the child grows up, and the man sleeps with her, I wanted to get a funny feeling there. I wasn't trying to be provocative or incestuous, but I did have an idea about how exciting it must be to see a man with a

nine- or ten-year-old girl, and you know that in so many years, he's going to lay her. That's what got me started on the yarn, because I like those sorts of stories: they get people nervous. I tried to get that in the picture, but I had to soft-pedal it. Today, I'd hit it. Oh, would I hit it! A hundred per cent.

The Steel Helmet—1950 (84 minutes)
Producer: Samuel Fuller. *Script:* Samuel Fuller. *Photography:* Ernest Miller. *Cast:* Gene Evans (Sergeant Zack), Steve Brodie (Lieutenant

Driscoll), James Edwards (Corporal Thompson), Robert Hutton (Soldier "Conchie" Bronte), Richard Loo (Sergeant "Buddhahead" Tanaka), Richard Monahan (Baldy), Sid Melton (Joe), William Chun ("Short Round"), Neyle Morrow (first G.I.).

Fixed Bayonets—1951 (92 minutes)

Producer: Jules Buck. *Script:* Samuel Fuller, from the story by John Brophy. *Photography:* Lucien Ballard. *Cast:* Richard Basehart (Corporal Denno), Gene Evans (Sergeant Rock), Michael O'Shea (Sergeant Lonergan), Richard Hylton (Wheeler), Skip Homeier ("Belvedere" Whitey), Richard Monahan (Walowicz), Don Orlando (Borcellino), Neyle Morrow (Medic).

Park Row—1952 (83 minutes)

Producer: Samuel Fuller. *Script:* Samuel Fuller. *Photography:* Jack Russell. *Cast:* Gene Evans (Phineas Mitchell), Mary Welch (Charity Hackett), Bela Kovacs (Ottmar Mergenthaler), Herbert Heyes (Josiah Daveport), Don Orlando (Mr. Angelo), Neyle Morrow (Thomas Guest).

The main ambition of Phineas Mitchell (Gene Evans) is to found a newspaper free of corruption, a paper that will give people the truth. He scrapes together all the money and help he can get and founds *The Globe.* One of the paper's first crusades is to raise money to complete the construction of the Statue of Liberty. Charity Hackett (Mary Welch), Mitchell's main competitor, accuses him of fraud and tries to drive him into a merger with her paper. He resists all her efforts and she finally concedes the battle.

Fuller: Did you like the street? That whole set was based on memory. It was authentic. I wanted it to look exactly like Park Row as I remembered it. It was very expensive. That picture still hasn't paid for itself. For example, I made them build the set four stories high, because that's how it really looked. Usually, you don't even build two stories. They said, "What do you want four stories for? You'll probably never even show it that high up. Nobody'll know it's there." I said, "I'll see it, and I'll know it's there. It means something to me. When I look up, I want to know it's there, all four stories." A lot of inside stuff is in the picture. Newspaper stuff. Little things that most people wouldn't notice. But I wanted it there.

Pickup on South Street—1953 (80 minutes)

Producer: Jules Schermer. *Script:* Samuel Fuller, from the story by Dwight Taylor. *Photography:* Joe MacDonald. *Cast:* Richard Widmark (Skip McCoy), Jean Peters (Candy), Thelma Ritter (Moe Williams), Richard Kiley (Joey), Milburn Stone (Winoki), Stuart Randall (Police Commissioner), Victor Perry (Lightnin' Louie). Won Venice Film Festival Bronze Lion Award.

Fuller accepting the Venice Film Festival Award.

Hell and High Water—1954 (103 minutes)

Producer: Raymond A. Klune. *Script:* Samuel Fuller, Jesse Lasky, Jr. *Photography:* Joe MacDonald. *Cast:* Richard Widmark (Adam Jones), Bella Daryl (Denise Gerard), Victor Francen (Professor Montel), Cameron Mitchell ("Ski" Brodski), Gene Evans ("Chief" Holter), David Wayne ("Dugboat" Walker), Don Orlando (Carpino), Neyle Morrow.

Professor Montel (Victor Francen), the scientist leader of a world pacifist organization, enlists the help of Adam Jones (Richard Widmark) to lead a submarine mission with the purpose of discovering and destroying a secret Asian atomic power plant. The professor accomplishes his purpose, although he is blown up along with the power plant.

Fuller: One kick I got out of the film: I had an idea for an underwater sequence in which I could use two submarines as two human beings. I said to Ray Kellogg, my special-effects man, "We pretend they're two dogfaces, two infantrymen." The most dangerous thing in the world is when you know that the fellow on the left or right of you has gone. It's pitch black out. You're waiting. You know you can't hear him return. Then you hear someone breathing. You know it's not your breathing. You can't see a thing. You hold your breath, and the enemy, who may be five or six feet away, holds his breath. When you exhale, you try to do it silently, and the more you try, the more you think it sounds like a rumble of thunder.

I said to Kellogg, "I want to get that effect with two submarines. They both play possum on the ocean bottom." Now, forget submarines. These are two men. Which man will breathe first? Which man will move first? Finally, one man says, "The hell with it. It's dark. I can't see. I'm going to strike out." That's what you do. Just strike out! And you shoot the son of a bitch. Only instead of this, in the picture, one submarine rams the other.

I also liked the scene where the plane is taking off at the end, and everybody shoots at it from the deck. I staged that specifically as a ballet: the light weapons, the medium weapons, and the heavy weapons. I swung my camera around so that it would look like a ballet. Because in war, when you see everyone firing, it is a ballet. It's a horrifying ballet.

House of Bamboo—1955 (102 minutes)
Producer: Buddy Adler. *Script:* Harry Kleiner. *Dialogue:* Samuel Fuller. *Photography:* Joe MacDonald. *Cast:* Robert Ryan (Sandy Dawson), Robert Stack (Eddie Spanier), Shirley Yamaguchi (Mariko), Cameron Mitchell (Griff), Sessue Hayakawa (Inspector Kita), Brad Dexter (Captain Hanson), Harry Carey, Jr. (John), Neyle Morrow (Corporal Davis), Samuel Fuller (Japanese police officer killed in final scene).

Run of the Arrow—1957 (85 minutes)

Producer: Samuel Fuller. *Script:* Samuel Fuller. *Photography:* Joseph Biroc. *Cast:* Rod Steiger (O'Meara), Sarita Montiel (Yellow Moccasin), Brian Keith (Captain Clark), Ralph Meeker (Lieutenant Driscoll), Jay C. Flippen (Walking Coyote), Charles Bronson (Blue Buffalo), Stuart Randall (Colonel Taylor), Neyle Morrow (Lieutenant Stockwell), Chuck Hayward (the corporal), Chuck Roberson (the sergeant).

China Gate—1957 (97 minutes)

Producer: Samuel Fuller. *Script:* Samuel Fuller. *Photography:* Joseph Biroc. *Cast:* Gene Barry (Brock), Angie Dickinson (Lia), Nat "King" Cole (Goldie), Paul Dubov (Captain Caumont), Lee Van Cleef (Major Cham), Neyle Morrow (Leung).

Forty Guns—1957 (79 minutes)

Producer: Samuel Fuller. *Script:* Samuel Fuller. *Photography:* Joseph Biroc. *Cast:* Barbara Stanwyck (Jessica Drummond), Barry Sullivan (Griff Bonnell), Dean Jagger (Ned Logan), John Ericson (Brockie Drummond), Gene Barry (Wes Bonnell), Robert Dix (Chico Bonnell), Paul Dubov (Judge Macy), Eve Brent (Louvenia Spanger), Chuck Roberson (Swain), Chuck Hayward (Charlie Savage), Neyle Morrow (Wiley).

Verboten—1958 (87 minutes)

Producer: Samuel Fuller. *Script:* Samuel Fuller. *Photography:* Joseph Biroc. *Cast:* James Best (Sergeant David Brent), Susan Cummings (Helga Schiller), Tom Pittman (Bruno Eckart), Paul Dubov (Captain Harvey), Neyle Morrow (Sergeant Kellog).

The Crimson Kimono—1959 (82 minutes)

Producer: Samuel Fuller. *Script:* Samuel Fuller. *Photography:* Joseph Biroc. *Cast:* Victoria Shaw (Christine Downes), Glenn Corbett (Detective Charlie Bancroft), James Shigeta (Detective Joe Kojaku), Anna Lee (Mac), Paul Dubov (Casale), Neyle Morrow (Hansel).

Underworld, U.S.A.—1960 (99 minutes)
Producer: Samuel Fuller. *Script:* Samuel Fuller. *Photography:* Hal Mohr. *Cast:* Cliff Robertson (Tolly Devlin), Dolores Dorn (Cuddles), Beatrice Kay (Sandy), Paul Dubov (Gela), Robert Emhardt (Connors), Larry Gates (Driscoll), Richard Rust (Gus), Gerald Milton (Gunther), Allan Gruener (Smith), David Kent (Tolly as a boy of 12), Peter Brocco (Vic Farrar), Neyle Morrow (Barney).

Merrill's Marauders—1962 (98 minutes)
Producer: Milton Sperling. *Script:* Milton Sperling and Samuel Fuller. *Photography:* William Clothier. *Cast:* Jeff Chandler (General Frank Merrill), Ty Hardin (Lt. Lee Stockton), Peter Brown (Bullseye), Andrew Duggan (Maj. George Nement), Will Hutchins (Chowhound), Claude Akins (Sgt. Kolowicz), Chuck Hayward (Officer), Chuck Roberson (American officer and Japanese guard).

Shock Corridor—1963 (101 minutes)
Producer: Samuel Fuller. *Script:* Samuel Fuller. *Photography:* Stanley Cortez. *Cast:* Peter Breck (Johnny Barrett), Constance Towers (Cathy), Gene Evans (Boden), James Best (Stuart), Hari Rhodes (Trent), Larry Tucker (Pagliacci), William Zuckert (Swanee), John Mathews (Dr. Cristo), Chuck Roberson (Wilkes), Paul Dubov (Dr. Menkin), Neyle Morrow (Psycho), Rachel Romen (Singing Nymphomaniac). Won Valladolid Human Interest Award in Spain.

The Naked Kiss—1964 (90 minutes)
Producer: Leon Fromkess, Sam Firks, Samuel Fuller. *Script:* Samuel Fuller. *Photography:* Stanley Cortez. *Cast:* Constance Towers (Kelly), Anthony Eisley (Griff), Michael Dante (Grant), Virginia Grey (Candy), Karen Conrad (Dusty), Barbara Perry (Edna), Neyle Morrow (Officer Sam), Charlie (Charlie).

Shark—1969
Producer: Skip Steloff, Mark Cooper, Jose Luis Calderon. *Script:* Samuel Fuller. *Photography:* "Hijo Mio." *Cast:* Burt Reynolds (Caine), Barry Sullivan (Mallare), Arthur Kennedy (The Doctor), Silvia Pinal (The Woman), Enrique Lucero (The Policeman).

CATALOG OF FILMS AND FILM DISTRIBUTORS

Many of the films discussed in this book are available in 16mm for film societies and colleges. Also, most of the films are available for television broadcasting (16mm and 35mm). Following is a list of films and various distributors. Catalogues and rental prices can be obtained from the distributors upon request.

	TV	16MM
ABRAHAM POLONSKY		
Force of Evil	NTA	BUD, WILL
BUDD BOETTICHER		
The Bullfighter and the Lady	HOL	AUD, FI, STA
The Magnificent Matador	TRI	AUD, BUD, COM, MOD, WILL
The Killer Is Loose	UAA	
Seven Men from Now	WB-7A	
The Tall T	SG	
Decision at Sundown	SG	BUD, MOD
Buchanan Rides Alone	SG	BUD, ICS, MOD, SWA, TFC, TWY
Ride Lonesome	SG	
Westbound	WB-7A	
Comanche Station	SG	COL, ICS, MOD, ROA, SWA, TFC
The Rise and Fall of Legs Diamond	WB-7A	

PETER BOGDANOVICH
(films referred to)

High Sierra	UAA	BRA, TW, WILL
Strangers on a Train	WB-7A	
North by Northwest	MGM-TV	BRA, FI
Psycho	PAR-TV	BRA, FI (*withdrawn 1968*)
Targets		FI (*available early 1970*)

ARTHUR PENN

The Left-Handed Gun	WB-7A	AUD
The Miracle Worker	UAA	UAS
Mickey One	SG	ARG, AUD, BRA, MOD, TW, TWY
The Chase	SG	ARG, AUD, BRA, MOD, MOT, TW, TWY

SAMUEL FULLER

I Shot Jesse James	PRI	BUD, ICS, MOD, WC
The Baron of Arizona	FIC	BUD, TFC, UC
The Steel Helmet	FIC	BUD, CWF, ICS, MOD, WILL
Fixed Bayonets	WB-7A	
Park Row	UAA	UAS, WC
Pickup on South Street	WB-7A	WILL
Hell and High Water	WB-7A	FI
The House of Bamboo	WB-7A	FI
Run of the Arrow	SEC	AUD
China Gate	NTA	ARG, MOD, WILL
Forty Guns	WB-7A	FI
Verboten	SEC	
The Crimson Kimono	SG	
Underworld, U.S.A.	SG	COL
Merrill's Marauders	WB-7A	
Shock Corridor	AA	AUD
The Naked Kiss	AA	

ADDRESSES OF DISTRIBUTORS

TV:

A A
Allied Artists Television
230 West 41 St.
New York, N.Y. 10036

17032 Burbank Blvd.
Encino, Calif.

1000 N. Lake-
shore Dr.
Chicago, Ill.

F I C
Film Investment Corp.
5912 W. Olympic Blvd.
Los Angeles, Calif. 90036

H O L
Hollywood Television Service
8530 Wilshire Blvd.
Beverly Hills, Calif. 90211

MGM-TV
MGM-TV
1350 Sixth Avenue
New York, N.Y. 10019

10202 Washington
Blvd.
Culver City, Calif.

333 N. Michi-
gan Ave.
Chicago, Ill.

NTA
National Telefilm Associates
8530 Wilshire Blvd.
Beverly Hills, Calif. 90211

120 East 56 St.
New York, N.Y. 10022

PAR-TV
Paramount TV Ent.
5451 Marathon Blvd.
Hollywood, Calif. 90038

1501 Broadway
New York, N.Y. 10036

PRI
Prime TV Films
527 Madison Ave.
New York, N.Y. 10022

SEC
Screen Entertainment Co.
4440 Lakeside Dr.
Burbank, Calif.

SG
Screen Gems Inc.
711 Fifth Ave.   1331 N. Beachwood Dr.
New York, N.Y. 10022   Hollywood, Calif.
                        90028

TRI
Triangle Program Sales
717 Fifth Ave.   3600 Wilshire Blvd.   645 N. Michi-
New York, N.Y. 10022   Los Angeles, Calif.   gan Ave.
                                               Chicago, Ill.

UAA
United Artists Associated
729 Seventh Ave.   15130 Ventura Blvd.   520 N. Michi-
New York, N.Y. 10019   Sherman Oaks, Calif.   gan Ave.
                                               Chicago, Ill.

WB-7A
Warner Brothers-Seven Arts
200 Park Ave.   2915 La Cienega Blvd. 550 W. Jack-
New York, N.Y. 10017   Los Angeles, Calif.   son St.
                                               Chicago, Ill.

16MM:

ARG
Argus Films
1225 Broadway
New York, N.Y. 10024

AUD
Audio Film Center
34 MacQuesten Parkway So. 406 Clement St.
Mount Vernon, N.Y. 10550 San Francisco, Calif.
94118

BRA
Brandon Films   (Film Center Inc.)   (Western Cin-
221 West 57 St.   20 E. Huron St.   ema Guild)
New York, N.Y. 10019   Chicago, Ill. 60611   244 Kearney
                                               St., San Fran-
                                               cisco, Calif.
                                               94108

BUD
Budget Films
4590 Santa Monica Blvd.
Los Angeles, Calif. 90029

COL
Columbia Cinematheque
711 Fifth Ave.
New York, N.Y. 10022

COM
Community Sound
2325 San Jacinto
Houston, Texas

C W F
Clem Williams Films
623 Centre Ave.
Pittsburgh, Penn. 15219

F I
Films Inc.
38 West 32 St.   5625 Hollywood Blvd.   4420 Oakton
New York, N.Y. 10001   Hollywood, Calif.   St.
                        90028   Skokie, Ill.
                                                 60076

I C S
Institutional Cinema Service
29 East 10 St.   2323 Van Ness   203 N. Wabash
New York, N.Y. 10003   San Francisco, Calif.   Chicago, Ill.
                        94109   60601

M O D
Modern Sound Pictures
1410 Howard St.
Omaha, Neb. 68102

M O T
Mottas Films
1318 Ohio Ave. N.E.
Canton, Ohio 44705

R O A
Roa's Films
1696 N. Astor St.
Milwaukee, Wisc. 53202

STA
Standard Film Service
14710 W. Warren Ave.
Dearborn, Mich. 48126

SWA
Swank Motion Pictures
201 S. Jefferson Ave.   400 Montgomery St.
St. Louis, Mo. 63166   San Francisco, Calif.
                              94104

TFC
The Film Center
915 Twelfth St.
Washington, D.C. 20005

TW
Trans-World Films
332 S. Michigan Ave.
Chicago, Ill. 60604

TWY
Twyman Films
329 Salem Ave.
Dayton 1, Ohio

UAS
United Artists 16
729 Seventh Ave.
New York, N.Y. 10019

UC
Union County Film Service
128 Chestnut St.
Roselle Park, N.J. 07204

W C

West Coast Films
253 Minna St.
San Francisco, Calif.

W I L L

Willoughby-Peerless
115 West 31 St.
New York, N.Y. 10001

ERIC SHERMAN AND MARTIN RUBIN

Son of Hollywood director Vincent Sherman, Eric Sherman made an hour-length documentary film on Charles Lloyd while an undergraduate at Yale University where he was the Executive Director of the Yale Film Society. Following his graduation in 1968, he made a feature length color film based on Thomas Mann's "Mario and the Magician."

Martin Rubin served as the *New Journal*'s movie review editor and was Chairman of the Yale Film Society. His next project is a book on the American film-maker Douglas Sirk.